高职高专旅游大类专业新形态教材

酒店英语

鲍艳利　曹长波　主　编

沈言蓓　董　逸　副主编

清华大学出版社

北　京

内 容 简 介

本书根据酒店主要岗位服务流程编写而成,充分满足了酒店服务过程中对英语语言、服务礼仪和服务程序的要求,融合国际酒店服务精神,促进学生跨文化交际能力与国际酒店职业能力的培养,为酒店行业从业者拓展职业发展空间奠定了坚实的基础。

本书共 4 章 22 个单元,包括前厅、客房、餐饮、会展、康乐等部门的服务英语,每个单元均配有学习目标、情景导入、知识背景、服务对话、课后练习和课外知识扩展等内容,同时吸纳了当前行业创新服务趋势方面的内容。

本书配有相关的课程教学大纲、PPT、视频、教案、练习题及答案、试卷等。

本书可作为各类院校酒店管理与数字化运营专业、旅游管理专业的教材,也可作为旅游接待相关行业的培训用书。

图书在版编目(CIP)数据

酒店英语/鲍艳利,曹长波主编. —北京:清华大学出版社,2022.9(2024.7 重印)
高职高专旅游大类专业新形态教材
ISBN 978-7-302-61576-7

Ⅰ.①酒… Ⅱ.①鲍… ②曹… Ⅲ.①饭店-英语-高等职业教育-教材 Ⅳ.①F719.2

中国版本图书馆 CIP 数据核字(2022)第 145561 号

责任编辑:吴梦佳
封面设计:傅瑞学
责任校对:李 梅
责任印制:曹婉颖

出版发行:清华大学出版社
      网　　　址:https://www.tup.com.cn,https://www.wqxuetang.com
      地　　　址:北京清华大学学研大厦 A 座　　　　　　邮　　编:100084
      社 总 机:010-83470000　　　　　　　　　　　邮　　购:010-62786544
      投稿与读者服务:010-62776969,c-service@tup.tsinghua.edu.cn
      质量反馈:010-62772015,zhiliang@tup.tsinghua.edu.cn
      课件下载:https://www.tup.com.cn,010-83470410
印 装 者:三河市铭诚印务有限公司
经　　销:全国新华书店
开　　本:185mm×260mm　　　印　　张:10.5　　　字　　数:253 千字
版　　次:2022 年 9 月第 1 版　　　　　　　　　　印　　次:2024 年 7 月第 3 次印刷
定　　价:38.00 元

产品编号:095322-01

前　言

随着我国酒店业与国际接轨程度的进一步提升,酒店业人才更加迫切地需要通过英语水平的提升来增加自身的竞争力。本书作为无锡城市职业技术学院2017年教育部全国职业院校旅游类示范专业点、2015年江苏省高校品牌专业——酒店管理专业的核心课程《酒店英语》的配套教材,从酒店管理与数字化运营专业学生的实际需求出发,以酒店多个部门的真实服务情境为基础,根据高职酒店管理与数字化运营专业人才培养的目标,着眼于促进就业结构型矛盾的解决,以服务发展、促进就业为导向,以国际酒店服务精神和创新能力的培养为主线,注重启发式教育,促进学生跨文化交际能力与国际酒店职业素养的养成,力求为学生在酒店业拓展良好的发展空间奠定坚实的基础。

本书的主要特色如下。

1. 紧扣国标的教材定位

本书紧扣教育部《普通高等学校高等职业教育(专科)专业简介》和《高等职业学校酒店管理与数字化运营专业实训教学条件建设标准(征求意见稿)》,明晰对酒店英语课程的功能定位,立足于促进学生建立国际酒店英语服务思维,引导学生在国际交流合作的大背景下自觉对中外酒店消费者的消费心理和消费习惯进行分析,从而能够更好地遵循国际酒店行业服务模式,了解酒店服务创新模式。

2. 任务驱动的教学内容

本书在内容编写上采用任务驱动模式,体现"教、学、做、创"一体化教学理念,注重职业岗位的情景性,紧紧围绕酒店职业的真实岗位内容和要求设计项目任务和能力训练,使内容具有较强的针对性与实用性。

3. 校企合作、工学结合的开发思路

本书突出校企合作优势,深化产教融合,体现"校企结合、工学结合"的开发思路。本书编写小组由中外教师和多年从事酒店管理工作的人员组成,团队成员前往长三角地区多家五星级酒店,通过问卷调查、口头访谈等形式,对学生的岗位英语能力、酒店对岗位英语的教学需求及酒店相应岗位使用英语的频率等进行了实地调研。在本书的编写过程中,编写小组根据酒店行业发展及酒店不同岗位对英语能力的实际需求进行分析,并结合酒店实际岗位工作任务所需的知识、能力、素质等,以真实的工作任务及工作过程为依据整合、细化教材内容。

4. 新形态立体、丰富的教学呈现

为激发学生的学习积极性,本书充分考虑学生的阅读感受和体验,注重过程考核,辅以多媒体课件、二维码视频、精品课程网站等立体化教学资源,有助于学生确立职业发展目标,增强跨文化交流的能力,促进学生职业生涯发展。

本书主编鲍艳利为无锡城市职业技术学院副教授,曾主持、参与多项教育部、省、市级课题的研究,发表多篇 SCI、EI、中文核心论文。鲍艳利负责本书的总体规划、体例统筹与内容选定,并负责编写客房、餐饮、会展及康乐部门服务英语部分。本书主编曹长波为无锡城市职业技术学院旅游学院酒店管理与数字化运营系主任,多次指导学生参加国家级技能大赛并多次获得一等奖。曹长波负责本书教学方法的设定并编写前厅部分。本书副主编沈言蓓为无锡城市职业技术学院旅游学院酒店管理与数字化运营系教师,曾参编"十三五"创新示范教材 1 部,多次指导学生参加各级技能大赛并获奖,负责本书校对与教学资源的整合开发。本书副主编董逸和参编刘佳琦毕业于中国传媒大学英语专业。

本书获批《江苏省 2019 年高等学校重点教材立项建设项目》(苏高教会[2019]23 号)。本书旨在帮助酒店管理与数字化运营专业学生熟悉酒店各项英文服务的工作流程、服务规范和服务礼仪;掌握英文服务技能,提高英语听说能力和跨文化沟通能力,为职业领域的拓展打好基础;培养良好的职业道德、职业意识,建立英语思维模式,具备终身学习的能力和勇攀职业高峰的斗志。

由于编者团队水平有限,书中难免存在不足之处,敬请各位同人及读者批评、指正。

编　者

2022 年 4 月

课程介绍

3 分钟片花

目　录

Chapter 1　Front Office

上海浦东丽思卡尔顿酒店
The Ritz-Carlton Shanghai, Pudong

Front Office is a very important department in the hotel，making direct contact with guests. The main function of this department is reservation，guest service，check-in，check-out，cashier，foreign currency exchange，room assignment，inquiry，etc.

The Front Office is also considered as the "nerve center" of a hotel. As this department is located around the foyer area of the hotel and is visible to guests，patrons and visitors，they are collectively called "Front Office".

Unit 1

Room Reservation

Objectives

- Understand the working procedures for room reservations.
- Deal with the situation flexibly when the hotel is fully booked.
- Deal with reservation cancellations in a professional manner.

Lead-in

1. Think it over and share your ideas with your classmates.

One of the most important qualities of hotel staff is a real liking for people and a warm desire to help them. Discuss with your classmates and find some good ways to cultivate this quality.

2. Match the following room types with hotel rooms in the pictures below.

A. single room   B. double room   C. twin-bed room(standard room)   D. suite

(1) _____

(2) _____

(3) _____

(4) _____

Part I Background Knowledge

Job Description for Reservation Agent

A hotel is a "home away from home" for all travelling guests who need rest, food and drinks. The front office of a hotel is not only its "shop window" but also its "nerve center". Its staff's efficiency and attitude are of great importance to guests' vacation or business, and indeed to the hotel operation. The job of a reservation agent is mainly to respond to requirements from guests, travel agents, and referral networks concerning reservations by mail, telephone, telex, cable, fax, or through a central reservation system; to create and maintain reservation records—usually by date of arrival and alphabetical letters of confirmation, cancellations and modifications. Additional duties may include preparing the list of expected arrivals for the front office, assisting in preregistration activities when appropriate, and processing advance reservation deposits.

Part II Situational Dialogues

Dialogue 1 FIT Room Reservation by Telephone

Scene: Helen (H) is the reservationist of Wuxi Intercontinental Hotel. She is receiving a reservation call from a guest named Williams (W).

H: Wuxi Intercontinental Hotel, reservation desk, Helen speaking. How can I help you?

W: Yes, I'd like to book a room in your hotel.

H: Sure. May I have your name, please?

W: Henry Williams.

H: Okay, Mr. Williams. May I know your arrival and departure dates?

W: From October 1st to the 3rd.

H: Okay, Mr. Williams. What kind of room do you prefer? We have single rooms, double rooms, twin-bed rooms and various suites.

W: I'd like a double room, please.

H: How many people are there in your party, Mr. Williams?

W: Just my wife and myself.

H: We have double rooms with bath and double with shower. Which do you prefer?

W: Any differences?

H: Mr. Williams, a double room with bath is RMB 688 yuan per night. For a double with shower, it is RMB 618 yuan.

W: Then I will choose the one with bath, please.

H: Mr. Williams, may I have your contact number? We can contact you if it is necessary.

W: Sure. It is 001-415-578-7342.

H: Thank you, Mr. Williams. So you've made a reservation for you and your wife, a double room with bath from Oct. 1st to 3rd. And the room rate is RMB 688 yuan. The contact number is 001-415-578-7342. Am I correct?

W: Exactly! Thank you!

H: Anything else I can do for you, Mr. Williams?

W: No, that is all. Thank you!

H: My pleasure. Thank you for calling. We are looking forward to your coming. And have a nice day. Bye!

W: Bye-bye.

Dialogue 2　Group Reservation

Scene: Henry Williams (W) is calling the Reservations of Wuxi Intercontinental Hotel to reserve rooms for his colleagues. Helen (H) receives his request.

H: Wuxi Intercontinental Hotel. Reservation Desk. Helen speaking. How can I help you?

W: This is Henry Williams calling from Spring Travel Service.

H: Oh, Mr. Williams. What can I do for you this time?

W: We have a meeting group from the USA. And we need to reserve rooms for them in your hotel.

H: How many people are there in this group, Mr. Williams?

W: There will be 40 people in it.

H: For which dates, please?

W: They are arriving on 22nd July, Monday and leaving on 25th July, Thursday.

H: That will be 3 nights. What types of room would they like, Mr. Williams?

W: Twenty twin-bed rooms, please.

H: Any other requirements, Mr. Williams?

W: They are going to have a meeting in your hotel. So, could you arrange a conference room for them?

H: Sure. For when, please?

W: On the afternoon of 23rd July, from 2:30 p.m. to 5:00 p.m.

H: No problem. We can make it for you, but we charge RMB 300 yuan per hour for using the meeting room.

W: Oh, I see. Is there any discount on the group reservation?

H: The contracted room rate for twin-bed room is 588 yuan per night, including breakfast. Is it OK?

W: That's all right.

H: How are they arriving? Do you want us to offer picking-up service?

W: No, thanks. They are arriving by air. Our tour guide will meet the group at the airport.

H: Do you pay everything, Mr. Williams?

W: No. We'll give our guests vouchers and we pay the value only on the voucher. Other expense must be settled by the guests themselves.

H: Okay, Mr. Williams. You have booked 20 TWBs for the guests from the USA, from 22nd July to 25th July, and a meeting room for 23rd, from 2:30 to 5:00 p.m. Am I correct?

W: That's right.

H: We will send you a confirmation by fax within 2 days. May I have your fax number?

W: You may fax at 0510-58586688.

H: Thank you for calling, Mr. Williams. Have a good day!

Dialogue 3　Fully Booked

Scene: Henry Williams（W）is calling the Reservations of Wuxi Intercontinental Hotel to reserve a room. But there is no room for the date he needs. Helen（H）receives his request.

H: Good afternoon. Reservation Desk. How may I help you?

W: I'd like to book a single room for August 23rd.

H: Just a moment, please. I'm sorry, sir. All the single rooms are booked up for that day.

W: Oh, it's too bad.

H: Would you like to try other room types? We still have some double rooms available for that day.

W: No, thank you.

H: Would you like us to put you on our waiting list so that we can call you in case we have a cancellation?

W: It's very kind of you. But I have an important meeting on that day in your city.

H: I see, sir. Would you like us to find you a room in a nearby hotel?

W: Yes, please. Thank you so much.

H: May I have your name and phone number, please? We will inform you if the reservation is made.

W: Henry Williams. The number is 001-145-5768-3208.

H: Okay, Mr. Williams. I will call you back later when the reservation is done.

W: Thank you. I really appreciate your help.

H: My pleasure. Thank you for calling us. We are always at your service.

Dialogue 4　Adjustment of the Reservation

Scene: Helen（H）is the reservation clerk of Wuxi Intercontinental Hotel. She is receiving a call from a guest named Williams（W）, and he wants to make adjustment of his reservation.

H: Good evening. Wuxi Intercontinental Hotel. Reservations. How can I help you?

W: Good evening, I'm calling from Los Angles. I've booked two rooms from Oct. 2nd to 5th. I want to revise it.

H: Sure. In whose name is the reservation made?

W: Henry Williams.

H: Mr. Williams, let me check. Yes, we do have a reservation made by you. So what kind of adjustment do you want to make?

W: The meeting I'm going to attend in your city will last one more day than it has planned. I'll extend my stay for one more night.

H: Would you please hold the line for a moment? I'll check the booking record. Yes, Mr. Williams, you can have the room you reserved for one more day.

W: That's great. Thank you so much.

H: You're welcome. So the reservation is changed like this: the same room, the date will be from Oct. 2nd to 6th. Am I correct?

W: Yes, exactly.

H: Anything else I can do for you, Mr. Williams?

W: No, thank you.

H: Thank you for calling. We are looking forward to your coming.

Dialogue 5   Cancellation

Scene: Helen (H) is the reservation clerk of Wuxi Intercontinental Hotel. She is receiving a call from a guest named John Smith(S), and he wants to cancel the reservation he made for his boss.

H: Good morning. Wuxi Intercontinental Hotel. Reservation Desk. Helen speaking. How may I help you?

S: Yes. I'm calling to cancel a reservation, because the schedule has been changed for the bad weather.

H: It is okay. In whose name was the reservation made?

S: Henry Williams.

H: Could you spell the last name, please?

S: W-I-L-L-I-A-M-S.

H: And for which dates, please?

S: From November 5th to 7th.

H: Thank you, sir. May I know whether the reservation was made for yourself or someone else?

S: For my boss.

H: Then could I have your name and telephone number, please?

S: Yes. It's John Smith and the number is 001-2354-3788.

H: Thank you, Mr. Smith. I will cancel Mr. Williams' reservation for November 5th to 7th.

S: Thank you very much.

H: It's my pleasure. We look forward to serving you in another chance. Have a nice day. Goodbye.

S: Bye-bye.

Part III　Useful Expressions

1. Greet guests.

Good morning/afternoon/evening. Wuxi Intercontinental Hotel. Reservations. Helen Speaking. How can I help you/May I help you/Can I be of any service to you?

2. Inquire about the reservation information.

Could I have your name and phone number, please?

How many people are there in your party?

For how long are you going to stay in our hotel?

May I have your surname/your fax number/the way to contact you/your last name/credit card number/passport number?

3. Ask the guest to wait.

Hold the line, please.

One moment, please.

Let me check the reservation record. Please wait a minute.

4. Tell the guest the room rate.

We can offer a single room with bath at RMB 658 yuan per night.

We charge RMB 658 yuan for a double room per night.

5. Inquire about the arrival information.

Could I know your arrival date, please?

How are you arriving? Your flight number, please?

May I know the estimated time of your arrival?

Do you need pick up service?

6. Confirm the reservation.

Now let me confirm your reservation: you've booked a single room from Oct. 3rd to 6th/a double room/a twin-bed room with credit card guarantee/rooms by advance deposit reservation

7. Tell the guest that your hotel is fully booked.

I'm awfully sorry, but all the rooms are booked up.

We have no vacancies for the dates you need.

We are fully booked for those days.

Part Ⅳ   Activities

1. Vocabulary: Get the correct meanings and learn them by heart.

Words and Expressions	Meanings	Words and Expressions	Meanings
front office		arrival	
reservation		departure	
a home away from home		single room	
efficiency		double room	
personality		suite	
central reservation system		TWB	
confirmation		adjustment	
cancellation		room rate	
modification		vacancy	
selling status		acknowledgement	
credit policy		guaranteed reservation	
no show		PMS	

2. Role-play.

Situation 1: John Brown is calling Wuxi Taihu Hotel. He wants to book 3 twin-bed rooms for his colleagues from Oct. 2nd to 5th. You are the reservation agent. Answer the phone and help him to book the rooms.

Situation 2: John Brown comes to Wuxi Taihu Hotel. He wants to book a single room for himself from September 7th to 9th. But there is no single room available for those days in your hotel. You are the reservation agent, please help him to solve the problem.

3. Practical writing.

How to Write a Confirmation Letter

Reservation confirmation is an acknowledgement given by the hotel to guests for their room request and also the personal details given at the time of booking. A written confirmation states the intent of both parties and confirms important points of agreement like name, arrival and departure dates, number of guests' staying, room rate, type of room booked, number of rooms, picking-up details, details of deposit made, package details, etc. A confirmed reservation may be either guaranteed or non-guaranteed. Details on the confirmation letter are retrieved from the reservation record and manually updated or entered automatically with the help of PMS used by the hotel on to a specially designed reservation confirmation form. Confirmation letter may also include the cancellation and no-show polices of the hotel. And it's also about the retention charges, hotel standard check-in and check-out time, early morning/early arrival charges and late departure charges. There are many different types of formats used by hotels for confirmation letters. We offer you a sample which may help you better understand what are included in a confirmation letter. Here is a sample for you.

Reservation Confirmation

Reservation No: 20220801

Date:

Dear Mr. /Mrs. (Guest Name)

We are delighted that you have chosen(**Mention your hotel Name**) and we are pleased to confirm your reservation as follows:

Company name	
Name of the guest(s)	
Number of guest(s)	
Number of room(s)	
Arrival date	
Departure date	
Flight details /Arrival time	
Departure time	
Airport transfer	
Room category	
Mode of payment	
Room rate	

A. Arrival and departure policy.

Check-in: 1400 Hrs

Check-out: 1300Hrs

Early check-in is subject to availability. For guaranteed early check-in, rooms are to be reserved from the previous night. Rooms are held until 4 p.m. on the day of arrival unless guaranteed by a credit card or deposit.

B. Cancellation policy.

All cancellations should be done 72 hours prior to the day of arrival to be exempted from the cancellation charges. This is equivalent to 1 day's retention charges. All no-shows will also attract 1 day's retention charges. A non-refundable reservation fee of (**$ 00.00**) is billed to the credit card used to guarantee the room reservation.

C. Guarantee policy.

All bookings must be guaranteed at the time of reservation by credit card or advance payment. All major cards are accepted.

D. Photo identity.

All Guests are requested to produce the government approved photo identity card and valid passport and visa for foreign nationals upon arrival.

We look forward to welcoming you at(**Mention Your Hotel Name**)

Best Regards

Reservations

Part V　Further Reading

How to Introduce Yourself to Others

A. Eye contact.

Eye contact shows that you are engaged in the interaction. Eye contact is one way to connect with each other and shows that the other person has your attention. When you make eye contact, it shows that you are open and engaged.

If you're not comfortable looking straight into someone's eyes, stare at the point between the eyebrows; she won't notice the difference.

If you're in a group setting, make periodic eye contact with those around you.

B. Smile.

It is important to keep a genuine, bright smile when you meet a new person. Be genuinely happy to meet someone new and to share a positive experience and it will help create a genuine smile. Including the upper part of your face in your smile creates a more genuine and less fabricated smile.

C. Body language.

Use appropriate body language. Your body language should communicate that you are confident and at ease. Stand with your head high and your back straight, being careful not to slouch.

Unit 2

Bell Service

Objectives

- Greet guests with proper expressions warmly.
- Understand the working procedures of escorting guests to their rooms.
- Master special terms for bell service.

Lead-in

Match the pictures with the words given below.

A. bathroom   B. luggage storage   C. elevators

D. restaurant   E. thermostat   F. service guide

G. remote control

(1) _____

(2) _____

(3) _____

(4) _____

(5) _____

(6) _____

(7) _____

Part Ⅰ   Background Knowledge

Job Description for Bellboy/Luggage Porter

Bell desk is an extended arm of the front desk. There are many activities at the time of arrival, during the stay and at the time of departure of the guest, which cannot be carried out from the front desk but are essential.

The work for a bellboy is primarily to greet and welcome all guests and relieve guests of their luggage on arrival. Hospitality and welcome are demonstrated by bell boys at all times, and all guest requests are dealt with in a prompt and courteous manner. In addition to assisting guests with luggage, porters are also responsible to collect and distribute posts and parcels. And they also deal with general enquiries and ensure the lobby and forecourt areas are always clean and tidy.

Part Ⅱ   Situational Dialogues

Dialogue 1   Greetings

Scene: Bob (B) is the bellboy of Wuxi Intercontinental Hotel. He is greeting a guest named Williams (W) when his car pulls up in front of the hotel.

B: Good afternoon, sir. Welcome to our hotel.

W: Good afternoon.

B: (opening the trunk, taking out the baggage and looking at the name on the baggage tags) I'm the bellman, Williams. So, you have got altogether four pieces of baggage?

W: Yes, three suitcases and one briefcase.

B: Are there anything valuable or fragile in them?

W: No. Nothing valuable or fragile.

B: Then Let me carry the luggage for you and show you to the reception desk. This way, please.

B: I'll put your luggage by the post over there. The reception desk is just straight ahead.

W: I see. Thanks.

B: A bellman will show you to the room when you have finished checking in.

Dialogue 2　Show the Guest to the Room

Scene：When the guest（G）finishes checking in，the bellman（B）shows the guest to his/her room.

B：May I show you to the room and open the door for you?

G：Oh，thank you.

B：May I have your room card?

G：Here it is.

B：This way please，Mr. Williams.

G：Thank you very much.

B：Here is the lift. After you，please.

G：Why don't you have the fourth floor?

B：In China，the number 4 has the same sound as the word "death". People don't like this number，because it reminds them of death.

G：Oh，it's just like the No.13 in western countries.

B：Yes. So we don't have the 13th floor，too.

G：It's very considerate of you.

B：I'm glad to hear that. Let me introduce our hotel to you. If you want to try Chinese food，you can go to Sunshine Restaurant and Garden Restaurant. If you prefer western food，please go to Lobby Restaurant. Also available are a beauty salon，a barber shop，gym，and game room and Snooker room. Remember to show your room card to the waiter，and you will get free of charge for Gym.

B：Here is your room 1620，sir.（knock the door three times，and open the door for the guest）After you，please. Please insert your room card here to turn on power switch. May I put your luggage here? Please check your luggage again. By the way，may I open the curtain for you? Your room faces south and commands a good view of the lake.

G：Yes，how lovely it is! Thank you.

Dialogue 3　Introduce Rooms to Guests

Scene：The bellboy，Ham（H）is introducing the room facilities to Mr. Williams（W）.

H：Here is a bedside control panel. It controls light，air-conditioner，TV and so on. Here is the mini-bar. You can get some beverage from it，and the price list is here. Here are some coffee and tea. It is free of charge for you. You can enjoy it.

W：Oh，thank you.

H：If you want to watch TV，please press the TV button. The TV remote control is here，and you can choose the TV program. Our hotel offers paid-movie service. If you would like to enjoy it，please press the movie's button and choose your favorite movies.

W：I see.

H: Let me tell you how to use the telephone, Mr. Williams. For room to room calls, please just dial the room number. If you make a local call, please dial "9" first, and then the telephone number. If you make DDD (Domestic Direct Dial) calls, press "9" first, district code and the telephone number; if you make IDD (International Direct Dial) calls, dial "9" first, then state code, district code and the telephone number.

W: Oh, thank you. It's complicated.

H: Our hotel offers Internet service. Our WiFi password is WX 888. Here is a service directory of our hotel. I believe it is useful for you during your stay.

W: Thanks.

H: There is a safe box in the closet, and you can use it to keep your valuables. There is a piece of fire escape plan behind the door. The red point shows where you are now.

W: That's very helpful.

H: Let me tell you how to use the bath shower. Before you bathe, please put the bath mat into the bathtub which can prevent you from slipping. There is a string above the bathtub; you can hang your clothes up.

W: Thank you very much. You are really helpful!

H: You are welcome, Mr. Williams. If you need any assistance, please contact us. Our extension is "8". Hope you enjoy your stay with us!

Dialogue 4   Check out Luggage Service

Scene: Mr. Williams(W) is going to check out. He calls the front office. Helen (H) answers the phone, and then she sends a bellboy (B) to help Mr. Williams with the luggage.

H: Good morning, Helen speaking, what can I do for you, Mr. Williams?

W: I'm going to check out today. Can you send someone to help me with my luggage?

H: Sure, the bellman with luggage cart will arrive in your room in a few minutes.

W: Thank you!

(The bellboy comes to Mr. Williams' room.)

B: You are going to check out, Mr. Williams? Is all your luggage here? Let me help you.
(They leave the room and come to the lobby)

B: Cashier is over there; you can go there and check out.

W: Fine.

B: May I book a taxi for you, sir?

W: That is great!

(The guest has settled his hotel bill; the bellman sees him off at the lobby and helps him into the car.)

B: I hope you have enjoyed your stay here, sir.

W: Yes, quite pleasant.

B: All your luggage is here. And the taxi is waiting just outside.

W: Thanks a lot.

B：You're welcome. We look forward to seeing you again.

W：I will recommend your hotel to my friends for your good service.

B：It would be very nice of you to do it. We're always to be of help to you.

W：I really appreciate your help.

B：Thank you. Watch your steps，sir. Please get on the taxi.

W：Goodbye.

B：Bon voyage.

Part III   Useful Expressions

1. Welcome guests.

Good morning/afternoon/evening. Welcome to our hotel!

Welcome to our hotel，Mr. Williams. It is really nice to see you again.

Welcome to our hotel，Mr. Williams. How are you doing today?

2. Help guests open or close the car door.

Be careful as you step down.

Watch your steps，sir.

The ground is a little bit slippery.

3. Show the way to the reception desk.

This way，please. The reception desk is over there.

Watch out for the revolving door.

Reception desk is on your right/left. You won't miss it.

Follow me，please.

4. Reply when the guest says "thank you".

You're welcome.

Not at all. We are always at your service.

I'm glad to hear that，Mr. Williams.

It's my pleasure.

The pleasure is mine.

5. Offer help to the guest.

May I show you to your room?

Let me help you with your luggage.

May I help you with your suitcases，sir?

Leave the luggage to me. I'll get it up to your room.

Don't worry. We'll send you a bellboy in a minute.

Leave the letters to me. I'll get them delivered.

6. Bid farewell to the guest.

I hope you have enjoyed your stay here，sir.

All your luggage is here. Please check it again.

The taxi is waiting just outside.

Bon voyage!

Goodbye. Hope to see you again.

7. Help the guest park the car.

The garage is around the corner/at the end of the drive.

OK, no problem. Just leave it to me.

You may go to the reception desk first while I am parking the car.

I will return the key to you later.

Part Ⅳ   Activities

1. Vocabulary: Get the correct meanings and learn them by heart.

Words and Expressions	Meanings	Words and Expressions	Meanings
concierge		reconfirm	
bellboy		tag	
porter		considerate	
luggage		available	
check out		bedside control panel	
identification		air-conditioner	
room amenity		TV remote control	
storage		DDD (Domestic Direct Dial)	
personal item		IDD (International Direct Dial)	
extension		Internet service	
bathtub		courtesy	

2. Role-play.

Situation 1: John Brown is a regular guest of Wuxi Taihu Hotel. He comes again to this hotel for a business trip. The car pulls up in the driveway. A bellman comes to open the door for him and chat with him.

Situation 2: John Brown is calling the front office. He wants to check out and needs a bellman to help him with his luggage. Helen answers the phone and sends a bellboy Bill to deal with this.

3. Practical writing.

How to Write a Welcome Letter

The welcome letter can be described as a gesture of courtesy and consideration to somebody who joins your company's staff or neighborhood or someone who will take part in a social event you host or other special occasions. It's the loveliest way to show this person that you appreciate his/her interest, presence or efforts in doing something under your management.

This kind of letter can be formal or casual, depending on the situation. When you are welcoming a new member to your organization, for example, the document will be formal. A letter to someone new in your neighborhood would have a more casual tone. When you write a welcome letter, your goal is to break the ice between you and your new friend, classmate, neighbor, customer or employee, as well as to make a good impression. It's an opportunity to demonstrate how much you value him or her. They should feel at ease in their new environment, and be pleasantly surprised by your gesture of welcome.

The welcome letter has the same structure as an usual one, but depending on who you're writing to and why it will start with different salutations and follow either a reserved or relaxed tone.

Sample Letter

Dear Ms. Bristow,

Welcome to Alta Vista!

We understand you plan to reside here, and we're sure you will find Alta Vista a pleasant and friendly place to work and live in.

If there is anything we can do to help you, please don't hesitate to let us know. Our business requires we be well informed about local conditions, and we may be able to help you in several ways. We can provide you with a street map, a list of fine places to dine, local arts events, routes, and schedules, and we can answer any questions you have regarding Alta Vista.

If you want to use our services, we will welcome the opportunity to include you among our clients.

Sincerely,
(Your Name)

Part V Further Reading

How to Introduce Yourself to an Individual

A. Exchange names.

If the introduction is formal, say "Hello, I'm (**first name**)(**last name**)". If it's informal, say "Hi, I'm (**first name**)". Immediately after you've stated your name, ask for the other person's name by saying "What's your name?" in a pleasant tone. When you learn the other person's name, repeat it by saying "It's a pleasure to meet you, Pedro" or "Nice to meet you, Caroline."

Repeating the person's name will help you remember it, and give the introduction a more personal touch.

B. Offer a handshake or other culturally appropriate greeting.

Most cultures have a form of physical contact to accompany a greeting. In the United States, it is often a handshake. Be sure to keep the handshake brief and not too loose (floppy) or firm (bone-breaking).

Be aware of cultural differences. For instance, it is considered rude to firmly shake hands in China.

It is often appropriate to greet with a hug, especially if you're meeting a friend of a friend or an in-law. Hugs show more openness than a handshake. Women may prefer a hug to a handshake more often than men.

In many cultures, it is culturally appropriate to greet with a kiss. In South America, for instance, all women are greeted with one kiss, and in France, women are greeted with one kiss on each cheek. If you are unsure of the appropriate greeting, follow the other person's lead or watch how other people greet around you.

C. Ask questions.

It's important to show interest in the other person. Ask where she is from, what she does for a living, or ask about any common bonds you may have. Ask about what she loves to do and the passions she has in life. Show that you are engaged and interested in what she says.

You may tell a little bit of your background in order to engage conversation and share about yourself. Telling someone where you work or that you love rock climbing is appropriate and may lead to more conversation topics.

Don't take the opportunity to talk only about yourself. You will come across as selfish or uninteresting.

D. Close the conversation.

After you've met someone for the first time, you should end the conversation by restating that you enjoyed the meeting. If the interaction was formal, say something like "Mrs. Castro, I'm delighted to have met you. I hope we can talk again soon." If your conversation was informal, you can say "It was great meeting you, Harold. Hope to see you around."

Unit 3
Check-in Service

Objectives

- Master the specialized terms and expressions for check-in service.
- Understand the working procedures for check-in guests with reservations.
- Check in walk-in guests flexibly.

Lead-in

Match the pictures with the words given below.

A. ID card   B. room card   C. passport

D. voucher   E. bill   F. arrival list

(1) _____

(2) _____

(3) _____

(4) _____

(5) _____

(6) _____

Part I   Background Knowledge

Job Description for Front Desk Agent

A front desk agent represents the hotel to the guest throughout all stages of the guest's stay. He or she will determine a guest's reservation status and identify how long the guest will stay, help guests complete registration cards and then assign rooms, accommodating special requests whenever possible. A front desk agent also verifies the guest's method of payment and follows established credit-checking procedures, and places the guest and room information in the appropriate front desk racks and communicates this information to the appropriate hotel personnel.

Part II   Situational Dialogues

Dialogue 1   Checking in Guest with a Reservation

Scene: Mr. Williams (W) and his wife are at the reception desk of Wuxi Taihu Hotel. The receptionist, Helen(H) handles the check-in and answers the guests' questions.

H: Good evening, sir and madam. Welcome to our hotel. How can I help you?

W: Good evening. My name is Williams, Henry Williams. I reserved a room in your hotel by phone several days ago.

H: Let me check, Mr. Williams. A double room with bath for three nights. Am I correct?

W: Yes, a garden view room, if possible.

H: We have some nice rooms on the eleventh floor, if it suits you.

W: Thank you.

H: Great, Mr. Williams. May I see your passports?

W: Sure. Here you are, and this is my wife's.

H: Would you fill in this registration form, please?

W: OK. Is that all right?

H: Yes, thanks. According to our policy, you should pay 3000 yuan as a deposit. How are you going to pay, in cash or by credit card?

W: By Master card.

H: May I take an imprint of the card, please?

W: Certainly.

H: Thank you, sir. Please sign your name here. Your room is 1121 on the eleventh floor. Here is your room card and your breakfast coupons. You can have breakfast from 7:00 a.m. to 10:00 a.m. in the western restaurant on the second floor.

W: Thanks.

H: You are welcome. Just a minute, please. A bellman will show you to your room. I hope you will enjoy your stay here.

Dialogue 2　Checking in a Walk-in Guest

Scene: Henry Williams (W) comes to the reception desk of Wuxi Intercontinental Hotel. He wants a room to stay but he has no reservation. Helen (H) answers his request.

H: Good afternoon, sir. May I help you?

W: Yes, please. I've just arrived from Singapore. Could you let me have a room for a few days?

H: Have you made a reservation, sir?

W: I'm afraid not.

H: How many people do you have, please?

W: Just one. I'm alone. Could you arrange a single room with bath for me?

H: How long are you going to stay here, sir?

W: Three nights.

H: Just a moment, please. I have to check if there's a room available. Oh, Room 8108 is available, which commands a good view of Taihu Lake.

W: Great! I'll take it. How much do you charge?

H: The room rate is RMB 580 yuan per night.

W: OK. I'll take it.

H: Please show me your passport and fill in this registration form.

W: I'll take care of it.

H: Thank you. Would you please pay RMB 2560 yuan as a deposit, and how are you going to pay?

W: In cash. Here you are.

H: Thank you. This is the receipt, and here is the room card to Room 8108. The bellman will show you up with your baggage. I hope you will enjoy your stay with us.

W: That's very kind of you.

H: You are welcome, Mr. Williams. If you need any help, do let us know.

Dialogue 3　Checking in Guests with a Group Reservation

Scene: A tour group arrives at the hotel, and the tour leader, Mr. Wong (W) comes to the reception desk to check in. The receptionist (R) receives him.

R: Good morning, sir. May I help you?

G: Yes, please. We'd like to check in.

R: Do you have reservations?

G: Yes. The Shanghai CITS has booked 30 rooms for us.

R: Could you please tell me the name of your group?

G: The US Computer Society.

R: Just a moment, please. (The receptionist checks the computer.) Yes, 30 twin rooms for three nights. And you've already paid a deposit for your rooms.

G: That's right. Here is the name list with our group visa.

R: Thank you. Here are the keys to the rooms. Do you need morning call?

G: Yes, please. 8:00 a.m. for tomorrow morning and 7:00 a.m. for the rest of the days.

R: And here are the vouchers for your breakfast buffet. The breakfast will be served at the Lily Restaurant on the 4th floor from 7:00 a.m. to 10:00 a.m.

G: Thank you.

R: We are always at your service. We hope you will enjoy your stay with us.

Dialogue 4　Extending the Stay

Scene: Mr. Williams (W) calls the front desk from Room 3816. He requires extending his stay. Helen (H), the receptionist answers his request.

H: Good morning! Front desk, Helen speaking. How may I help you?

W: Good morning! I want to extend my stay for one more night due to my errand.

H: Just a moment, please. May I have your name and room number, please?

W: Williams, Room 3816.

H: Wait for a second, Mr. Williams. I'll check our room availability. Sorry to have kept you waiting, sir. I'm afraid our single rooms are fully booked. Would you mind a double instead?

W: OK. I will take it. Any price differences?

H: A double with bath is RMB 586 yuan, which is a little more expensive than the single.

W: No problem. I'll take it.

H: In this way, you may have to come to the front desk to go through the formality so that we can have a room changed for you.

W: I will do that after my breakfast.

(one hour later ...)

W: Hello. My name is Williams, Room 3186. I have called the front desk to extend my stay for one more night.

H: Yes, Mr. Williams, we will help you move to room 5816 and the room rate is RMB 586, including 15% service charge. Will that be fine?

W: Just fine.

H: You have deposited RMB 1000 yuan, and it is necessary to add RMB 1000 yuan as an additional deposit.

W: Here is my credit card.

H: Thanks. Please sign your name here. And here is your new room card. Please give the room card of Room 3186 back to me. Hope you have a nice stay.

W: Thank you.

Part III   Useful Expressions

1. Inquire about the reservation status.

Do you have a reservation?

Have you made a reservation?

Have you reserved a room?

Have you booked any rooms in our hotel?

2. Ask the guest to register.

Would you like to register now?

Will you please fill in this registration form?

May I have your passport?

Would you mind filling out this registration form?

Please sign your name on this registration form.

3. Help the guest finish the registration form.

Please fill out your nationality, permanent address, passport number, and visa number.

Would you mind signing your name here?

I need your signature here.

4. Greet regular guests.

Nice to see you again, Mr. Williams.

How have you been, Mr. Williams?

How are you doing today, Mr. Williams?

Haven't seen you for a long time. How are you getting along these days?

5. Help guests extend their stay.

You want to extend your stay, don't you?

So you need to extend 2 days for your stay. Am I right?

How many nights would you like to extend?

Just a moment, please. I'll check our room availability for the next three days.

You need to go through the formality later.

6. Ask the guest to make the payment.

How will you pay?

How will you make your payment?

How would you like to settle your bill?

How are you going to pay, sir? In cash, by credit card or with traveler's checks?

7. Show your good wishes to guests.

I hope you will enjoy your stay here!

Please enjoy your stay here!

Hope you will enjoy your stay!

Have a nice day!

Part IV   Activities

1. Vocabulary: Get the correct meanings and learn them by heart.

Words and Expressions	Meanings	Words and Expressions	Meanings
registration		bill	
reservation status		invoice	
assign		escort	
payment		ID card	
hotel personnel		garden view room	
service charge		passport	
room status		receptionist	
visa		extend the stay	
permanent address		go through the formality	
safe deposit box		room card	
nationality		travel agent	

2. Role-play.

Situation 1: Peter Anderson reserved a deluxe single room yesterday in Wuxi International Hotel. Now he comes to the front desk to check in. You are the receptionist and offer service to him.

Situation 2: John Brown comes to the front desk and wants to extend his stay for two more nights. But his room is already reserved by another guest for those days. You are the receptionist, please help him to solve the problem.

3. Practical writing.

Guest Registration Card

After the guest arrives at the hotel, the front desk agent creates a guest registration record in order to collect important guest information such as full name, address, date of birth, email, telephone number, company name, passport and visa details. Registration card may also include details of the reservation, such as room type, room rate, billing instructions, arrival and departure dates etc. In some countries, it is a legal requirement to have the guest signature on the registration card. Even in hotels with fully automated front office management systems guests may be asked to sign on the pre-printed registration card on arrival as a legal requirement. We offer you a sample which may help you better understand what is included in a registration card. You may fill in this registration card with your own information.

Sample

Welcome to Wuxi International Hotel

Confirmation Number：

Arrival Date：	**Departure Date：**
Arrival Time：	**Departure Time：**
Number of Rooms：	**Rate：**
Number of Adults：	**Number of Children：**

Guest Name：

Company/Travel Agent：

Email Address：

Mobile Number：

Terms and conditions：

（1）Check-in time is from 14：00 and check-out time is until 12：00.

（2）The guest acknowledges joint and several liabilities for all services rendered until full settlement of bills.

（3）Guests will be held responsible for any loss or damage to Halcyon House caused by themselves, their friends or any person for whom they are responsible.

（4）Hotel management is not responsible for your personal belongings and valuables like money, jewellery or any other valuables left by guests in the rooms.

（5）Complimentary safe deposit boxes subject to the terms and conditions for use are available in rooms.

（6）Regardless of charge instructions, I acknowledge that I am personally liable for the payment of all charges incurred by me during my stay at (**Mention Hotel Name**).

Guest Signature：	
Date：	**Check-in by Staff：**

Part V Further Reading

How to Introduce Yourself at a Professional Event

A. Say your full name.

Make sure you provide your full name so that the person can remember your name. You can say, "Hi, my name is Mark Salazar," or "Hello, I'm Angela Grace," and they'll be more likely to remember you.

B. Give a one-sentence description of what you do.

If you're at a networking event, then it's likely that you'll be talking about what you do to a variety of people. Unless you're having a more lengthy conversation, you should be prepared to give a one-sentence description of what you do that gives the following information.

Who are you, professionally? Are you a teacher, a project manager, or a health care professional? Who do you work with? Do you work with children, cross-cultural project teams, or micro-finance organizations?

Now, put your sentence together. State who you are, who you work with, and what you do.

C. Respect people's space.

If you have items, don't place them on the recruiter's or presenter's tables. Respect their space and don't overwhelm them. You may disrupt their materials, such as knocking over a poster or messing up pamphlets. Wait to be asked to exchange business cards, resumes, etc.

D. Follow up with a question.

If the person has asked you what you do first, don't just walk away and praise yourself for a job well done. Instead, ask the person what he or she does in return. This is not only polite, but shows that you have a real interest in this person's career path and want to build a meaningful connection.

E. Say goodbye like a professional.

Don't just wave and say, "Nice meeting you" and walk away from the person. Anyone you meet at a networking event can have the potential to help you in the future, so make sure that you make eye contact, repeat the person's name, and exchange business cards or any other pieces of relevant information before you walk away.

Unit 4

Concierge Service

Objectives

- Use the specialized terms and expressions for concierge service.
- Know the duties of a concierge.
- Understand the qualifications of a concierge.

Lead-in

1. Discuss with your classmates.

Have you ever enjoyed good concierge service at a hotel? What do you think of the importance of a concierge?

2. Match the pictures with the words given below.

A. golden keys   B. trolley   C. concierge

D. roll abroad   E. briefcase   F. trunk

(1) _____

(2) _____

(3) _____

(4) _____

(5) _____

(6) _____

Part I Background Knowledge

Job Description for Concierge in a Hotel

In the service industry, the word "concierge" was first used by Mr. Ferdinand Gillet, who founded Les Clef d'Or in Paris, France in 1929. Les Clef d'Or is the oldest surviving personal, professional, international network service industry organization in the world. It has no religious or political affiliation, but is solely focused on a genuine desire to serve hotel guests around the world. The concierge serves a valuable function in larger, and sometimes more upscale hotels. The ideal concierge should be friendly, outgoing, helpful, courteous, knowledgeable, and professional.

The main jobs for them are to serve as the guest's liaison to both hotel and non-hotel services. Their functions are an extension of front desk agent duties. They will assist the guest—regardless of whether inquiries concern in-hotel or off-premises attractions, facilities, services, or activities. They know how to provide concise and accurate directions, make reservations and obtain tickets for flights, the theatre, or special events and can organize special functions such as VIP cocktail receptions, and arrange for secretarial services. Also, they have thorough knowledge of property management software (PMS) or hotel reservation software.

Part II Situational Dialogues

Dialogue 1 Receiving Guests at the Airport

Scene: Bill (H) is the airport representative of Wuxi Intercontinental Hotel. He is receiving a guest named Williams (W) from USA at Wuxi Shuofang International Airport.

B: Excuse me, but are you Mr. Williams from the ABC Company of the United States?

W: Yes, my name is Henry Williams.

B: It's really nice to see you, Mr. Williams. I'm Bill Richard, the airport representative from Wuxi Intercontinental Hotel. I'm here to meet you.

W: Thank you so much.

B: You are welcome, Mr. Williams. How was your flight?

W: It's pretty well.

B: I'm glad to hear that, Mr. Williams. Welcome to Wuxi. By the way, have you ever been to our city before?

W: No, it is my very first time to be here.

B: I do hope you will enjoy it.

W: I'm sure I will. I've heard of it long before. It is really a nice place to stay.

B: Is all your luggage here, Mr. Williams?

W: Yes, one suitcase and one briefcase.

B: Let me carry the baggage for you.

W: Thank you so much, but I can manage the briefcase myself.

B: Pleasure is mine, Mr. Williams. We have a car over there to take you to our hotel. This way, please.

W: Great!

Dialogue 2   Buying Concert Tickets for Guests

Scene: Mr. and Mrs. Williams are free tonight, so they intend to go to a concert. Now Mrs. Williams (W) is talking with a concierge (C) about it.

C: Good afternoon, Mrs. Williams. Can I be of any service to you?

W: Good afternoon. Are you able to get me two tickets to a concert in this area tonight?

C: I will certainly do my best. What kind of concert would you like to attend?

W: Classical or pop.

C: All right. I can get you tickets to the symphony tonight, if you don't mind sitting on the balcony level.

W: That would be wonderful. I'll take the symphony balcony tickets. Would you mind finding out for me tonight's symphony program as well?

C: Certainly. I will call you within the next hour. What is your room number?

W: I'm in 1019.

C: Thank you, Madam. I do hope that we can assist you.

Dialogue 3   Recommending Local Restaurant

Scene: Mr. and Mrs. Williams have been staying at Wuxi International Hotel for several days. They decide to enjoy the local delicious food today, but they are not very familiar with the local food. So Mr. Williams (W) comes to the concierge (C) desk to ask for some advice.

C: Good morning. What can I do for you, Mr. Williams?

W: Well, I wonder if you could recommend a good local restaurant to us. My wife and I want to try some local Chinese dishes.

C: Certainly, sir. As far as I know, there is no other place in the whole city that certainly pleases your appetite better than the A'fu Restaurant. The restaurant serves very good and traditional local dishes. You might want to try there.

W: How far is it from here?

C: It is located in Guanshan Road, and a little bit far from here. I would suggest that you take a taxi there.

W: Shall I make a reservation for the dinner?

C: That will be better. The restaurant usually is crowded with clients at nights. Tell me the time you will have the dinner; I can make the reservation for you.

W: Thank you. Around 6 p.m.

C: OK. I'll make it done in 10 minutes.

W: One more thing, do you mind writing down the name of the restaurant on this piece of paper so that I can show it to the taxi driver?

C: Yes. Here you are.

W: By the way, do you have any idea how much we should pay the taxi driver for the trip?

C: RMB 25 to 30 yuan would be plenty to cover it. That's about three U.S. dollars.

W: Thank you for the information. Have a nice day.

C: The pleasure is mine. Enjoy your meal.

Dialogue 4　Booking Flight Tickets

Scene: Bill (B) is the concierge clerk of Wuxi Intercontinental Hotel. A guest named Williams (W) comes to the concierge desk to ask Bill to help him booking flight tickets.

B: Good evening, how can I help you this time, Mr. Williams?

W: Good evening. I'm flying back to Los Angles. I hope you can book an airline ticket for me.

B: Sure, Mr. Williams. For when, please?

W: For Oct. 8th.

B: Wait for a second, Mr. Williams. Let me check the computer. There are several flights to Los Angles for that day. When would you like to leave?

W: I want to catch a flight in the afternoon, so I can get home in the next morning.

B: I see, Mr. Williams. What about the flight around 5 p.m.?

W: That will be fine.

B: OK. I will check it for you with the airport booking office right away.

W: Thank you. When could I get my ticket?

B: We'll let you know if the ticket is available one hour later by phone. If it is done, please come again for the ticket when it's convenient for you.

W: Pretty well.

B: Is there anything else I can do for you, Mr. Williams?

W: No, thank you. You are really helpful.

B: My pleasure.

Dialogue 5　Booking a Tour for Convention Group

Scene: A meeting organizer (O) comes to the concierge to book a tour in the local scenic spot. Bill(B) helps him.

B: Good morning, sir. How can I help you?

O: Yes. I'd like to book a city tour for my group. They are just having a convention in your hotel.

B：Sure. Could I know the convention's name?

O：International Conference on Environmental Protection.

B：Let me see. So there are 40 people in your group. Will they all take the tour?

O：Yes，they will all join the tour.

B：In that case，you need a large limousine. When would you like to go?

O：In the morning on the day after tomorrow. They will finish the meeting tomorrow.

B：Which scenic spot would you like to go? There are many places of interest in our city.

O：Do you have any recommendations?

B：While I think the Turtle-head Park is worthy of visiting. Huishan Ancient Town is also a good place to go.

O：OK. I think I'll take Huishan Ancient Town.

B：Do you need a tour guide to serve you all through the tour?

O：Certainly. And the guide must be capable of speaking English.

B：No problem.

O：How much do you charge for all the service?

B：Let me see. The limousine，the guide，and the entrance fee … It totals 5000 yuan.

O：I'll pay by credit card.

B：Here is the timetable of the tour. The limousine leaves at 7：00 a.m. the day after tomorrow. The tour guide will contact you for further details later.

O：Thank you very much.

B：You are welcome. Have a wonderful tour！

Part Ⅲ Useful Expressions

1. Recognize a guest.

Excuse me，but are you Mr. Williams from the USA?

Excuse me，aren't you Mr. Williams from Canada Trading Company?

You must be Mr. Williams. Nice to meet you.

2. Inquire about the trip information.

What about your trip?

Do you have a pleasant trip?

Did you have a nice trip?

You must be tired after such a long flight.

How was your journey，sir?

3. Show good wishes to the guest.

I believe you will like our hotel.

I hope you will enjoy your stay here.

I wish you a pleasant stay with us.

Have a pleasant trip.

4. Introduce yourself.

I'm Bill Smith from Wuxi International Hotel.

I'm Helen from Sheraton Wuxi.

My name is Lily.

Call me Bill, please.

5. Introduce transportation information.

We have a limousine over there to take you to the hotel.

Our hotel shuttle bus in the parking lot will take you there.

This car will take you to our hotel directly.

It will take us 45 minutes to get to the hotel.

A taxi is expected to be here in 10 minutes.

6. Inquire about flight information.

Could I know which airline you prefer?

A flight leaves Wuxi at 7:15 a.m., arriving in San Francisco at 2:00 p.m. Will that be all right?

How many people are there in your travelling group?

7. Inform the guest of the result of flight booking.

I'll check that for you with the airport booking office.

We'll inform you as soon as we get the ticket.

We'll let you know the result in half an hour.

Please come to the concierge desk again at 5:00 p.m. and we'll let you know if the tickets are available.

Part IV Activities

1. Discussion.

Punctuality is a very important quality for the staff working as a concierge. But it doesn't come naturally to everyone. Discuss with your partners to find some good ways that you can train yourself to be on time.

2. Vocabulary: Get the correct meanings and learn them by heart.

Words and Expressions	Meanings	Words and Expressions	Meanings
concierge		itinerary	
Les Clef d'Or		entertainment	
genuine desire to serve		valet parking	
courteous		storage	
knowledgeable		safety guideline	

Continued

Words and Expressions	Meanings	Words and Expressions	Meanings
liaison		airport representative	
symphony		briefcase	
limousine		recommend	
attraction		airline ticket	
transportation		scenic spot	

3. Role-play.

Situation 1: John Brown is going to stay in Wuxi Taihu Hotel; he just gets off the plane and comes to the airport representative desk. You are the concierge agent and greet him there.

Situation 2: John Brown comes to the concierge desk of Wuxi Taihu Hotel and wants to book an airline ticket to San Francisco for the next morning. You are the concierge on duty that day.

4. Practical writing.

Paging Board

A paging board is always used by the hotel travel desk/concierge while picking up guests from the airport, railway station, bus terminals etc. This board has the name of the guest mentioned on it with details. We should pay attention to the following tips while preparing the paging board:

Double check the spelling, as no guest will like to see his/her name is wrongly spelt. The A4 paper used for placard printing should be clean, not crumpled and also stain-free. Always use the font size between 70 to 85 depending upon the length of the guest name. Here is a sample for you.

Sample:

> **Wuxi International Hotel**
>
> **WELCOMES**
>
> **Mr. John Brown**
> **ABS Trading Company**
> **FLIGHT: DUBAI TO LONDON [BA 1245] ETA: 1700**

Part V Further Reading

A Welcome Speech

Good afternoon, ladies and gentlemen. Welcome to China and our beautiful city,

Wuxi. I am your local guide. My Chinese name is Li Ming, and my English name is Sarah. You may call me Xiaoming. I think it is easier for you to remember. This is our driver Mr. Wang. He/She has ten years' driving experience in the travel industry. So we are in safe hands. Our bus number is Su B12345 and it is a big blue bus. Please remember our bus number. On behalf of China International Travel Service, I'd like to extend our warmest welcome to all of you.

Mr. Wang and I feel very honored to be at your service during your stay here. We will try our best to make your current trip a very pleasant one. If you have any questions or problems, please let us know. I will try my best to help you. Now everybody, please remember my cell phone number, 138888888888. Once again 13888888888. Call me if you need me.

I hope we will have a nice trip in the following two days here in Wuxi together. On the first day, we will visit Lingshan Grand Buddha and the Turtle-head Park, and on the second day we will go to the Xihui Park and try some local dishes.

Our bus is heading for the hotel. It will take us about 20 minutes to get there. The name of the hotel is Jinling Hotel. It is located on the Taihu Lake. You will find it a really nice place to stay. Well, ladies and gentlemen, now please sit and relax.

Unit 5

Operator Service

Objectives

- Memorize the specialized terms and expressions of operator service.
- Understand the working procedures of transferring messages.
- Provide a wake-up call service.

Lead-in

1. Match the pictures with the words given below.

　　A. mobile phone　　　　　B. operator　　　　　C. switchboard

　　　(1) _____　　　　　　　(2) _____　　　　　　　(3) _____

2. Discussion: What kinds of etiquette and skills should we have when we make phone calls with foreigners in English?

Part I　Background Knowledge

Job Description for Hotel Operator

　　As a hotel operator, you must speak clearly, distinctly, and with a friendly, courteous tone. You are able to use listening and speaking skills to put callers at ease and obtain accurate, complete information. You should answer incoming calls and direct them to guest rooms through the telephone console or to hotel personnel or departments. Also you have to take and distribute messages for guests, provide information on guest services, and answer inquiries about public hotel events.

Part II   Situational Dialogues

Dialogue 1   Leave a Message

Scene: Helen (H) is the operator of Wuxi Intercontinental Hotel. She is receiving a call from a guest named Williams (W).

H: Wuxi Intercontinental Hotel, operator speaking. How can I help you?

W: Yes, I'd like to call my friend. He told me he would stay in your hotel for recent days. Could you put me through?

H: Of course. May I have your friend's name and room number?

W: Henry Brown. His room number is 8018.

H: Okay, I'll put you through right away.

(There is no answer from Room 8018.)

H: I'm sorry, sir. It seems that Mr. Brown is not in his room at the moment. Could I leave a message for you?

W: Thank you very much. Could you tell him that Mr. Williams called him and asked him to call back when he gets back to his room? My number is 65456786.

H: OK. Mr. Williams is at 65456786. I will leave your message to Mr. Brown.

W: Thank you.

H: You are welcome. Have a good day.

Dialogue 2   Place Calls for the Guest

Scene: Henry Williams (W) is calling a local company which is his business partner. But he cannot understand Chinese from the switchboard of his partner's company. So he asks the hotel operator (Helen) to help him call his partner directly.

H: This is the operator. Helen speaking. How can I help you?

W: This is Henry Williams from Room 6018. I've tried to call a number in Wuxi but I can't understand what they said. Could you place the call for me?

H: Certainly, Mr. Williams. May I have the number you are calling?

W: 85976568.

H: 85976568. Is it a company or private number, Mr. Williams?

W: A company one.

H: May I know the company's name?

W: It is ABN Computer Company.

H: Who would you like to speak to, Mr. Williams?

W: Li Chen, the sales supervisor, please.

H: OK, Mr. Williams. You can hang up now, and I will call you back later when I get the phone through.

W: Thank you.

H: Pleasure is mine, Mr. Williams. Have a good day!

Dialogue 3 Arrange a Morning Call

Scene: Henry Williams (W) is calling the operator and he wants to be waken up the next morning. The operator, Helen (H), is answering the call.

W: Good evening! This is Williams in Room 303.

H: Good evening, Mr. Williams. What can I do for you?

W: I'm going to Shanghai early tomorrow morning. So I would like to request an early morning call.

H: Yes, Mr. Williams. At what time would you like us to call you tomorrow morning?

W: Well, I'm not really sure. But I have to be at the conference room of the Garden Hotel in Shanghai by 10 o'clock. You wouldn't know how long it takes to drive to Shanghai from the hotel, would you?

H: I would give it two to three and a half hours.

W: That means that I'll have to be on the road by 7 o'clock at the latest.

H: That's right.

W: Well, in that case, I would like you to call me at 5:45.

H: OK. So we will wake you up at 5:45 tomorrow morning. Good night, Mr. Williams. Have a sound sleep.

W: Good night.

Dialogue 4 Make a Long-distance Call

Scene: Mr. Frank (F) is calling the operator to see what's wrong with his long-distance. Lily (L) answers the phone and helps him solve the problem.

L: Good morning. Operator speaking. May I help you?

F: This is Frank from Room 1109. I have been trying to call my friend just now for several times, but failed. What's the matter with the phone?

L: Are you sure that you dialed his cell phone number correctly, Mr. Frank?

F: Absolutely. I checked it over twice in my phone book.

L: Did you dial "0" before you dialed his number?

F: No. What's "0" for? Why should I dial it first?

L: Well, you see. If you want to make a DDD call, you have to dial "0" to connect your phone with the hotel's DDD system.

F: Thank you. By the way, how is the long-distance call charged?

L: Our system will record the time automatically. We charge RMB 1 yuan per minute. We put the telephone fee on your expense account. You can pay it when you check out.

F：Oh，I see. Thank you.

L：You're welcome. Have a nice day. Bye.

Part Ⅲ　Useful Expressions

1. Help a guest with telephone service.

For room-to-room calls，please dial the room number directly.

For calls inside the city，please dial 9 first then the number.

For calls outside the city，dial 0 then the area code and the number，please.

For international direct-dial calls，dial international prefix first，then the country code，and the number.

2. Transfer calls.

Would you mind telling me which department he is working in?

Where would you like me to transfer your call?

I'll put you through.

I'll transfer your call to ...

May I put you through to Sales Department?

May I put you through to ... and they can help you.

3. Refuse the guest politely.

I'm afraid that the guest you are looking for is not registered.

I'm afraid you have the wrong room number.

May I put you through to reception to double check it for you?

I'm sorry，sir/madam. We wouldn't tell you the room number without the guest's permission.

He is not available at the moment. Would you like to leave a message or call back later?

4. Reply to the guest if nobody answers the call.

I'm sorry，sir/madam. There is no answer. Would you like to call back later?

There is no answer. Would you like me to connect you to the voice mail?

I'm sorry，but the line is busy.

5. Ask guests to leave a message.

May I take a message?

Would you like to leave a message?

May I have your name and telephone number，please?

Could you tell me the guest's room number?

May I have the guest's full name?

Could you tell me the message?

May I repeat the details for you?

6. Ask the guest if he/she wants to answer a call.

Good morning/afternoon/evening，Mr. /Ms. XX. This is XX from Guest Service

Center. Sorry to disturb you. Mr./Ms. XX is waiting for you on the line. Would you like to answer the phone?

The line is connected. Go ahead，please.

7. Arrange morning call service.

What time would you like your morning call?

Would you like the second time wake-up call?

Mr./Ms. XX，you'd like a 7:00 a.m. and a 7:10 a.m. morning call tomorrow for Room 502. After you wake up，you'd like a cup of green tea. Is it correct?

Good morning，Mr. XX，this is your 7:00 a.m. wake-up call. Coffee/tea is coming. Have a nice day!

Part IV Activities

1. Vocabulary：Get the correct meanings and learn them by heart.

Words and Expressions	Meanings	Words and Expressions	Meanings
operator		attitude	
switchboard		leave a message	
emergency call		wake-up call service	
Guest Service Center		health and safety	
Maintenance Department		paging board	
positive		country code	
vocal quality		area code	
DDD		international prefix	
IDD		dial	

2. Role-play.

Situation 1：Mr. John Jefferson is staying in Wuxi Intercontinental Hotel. His colleague Sam calls him for important business. But John is not in his room. So Sam asks the operator to leave him a message.

Situation 2：John Brown makes a call to ask for an arrangement of morning call service. You are the operator. Please help him.

3. Practical writing.

Handling Hotel Guest Messages and Message Format

In hotels，telephone messages are usually handled by the operator or by the hotel front office staff. They should be courteous and helpful when handing the incoming calls. Front office clerks often take phone messages for other employees or guests. They will have a standard telephone message form.

Here is an example of the message slip. Try to take a message for a guest in your hotel in this form. Here is a sample for you.

Sample:

SHERATON EST. 1937 ★★★★★	**Sheraton Wuxi Binhu Hotel**
Message For	(Guest name with salutation)
Room No.	(Guest room No.)
Date	(Date of creation of message)
Time	(Time of creation of message)
Created By	User who created this message
Message	

[place the message content here]

Part V   Further Reading

Telephone Etiquette for Hotel Staff

Regardless of whom you talk with over the telephone, it's essential that you make a positive impression. Answering the telephone is an opportunity for operators/front desk agents/hotel staff to portray a professional image as well as a positive image for the hotel. During any telephone conversations, hotel staff should follow the key points below:

Smile even though you are on the telephone. When you smile, you automatically improve your vocal quality, and you will also sound pleasant and interested.

Sit or stand up straight. By sitting or standing up straight, you'll be more alert and pay better attention to what is being said.

Use a low voice pitch. A lower voice pitch will make you sound more mature and authoritative.

Avoid expressions such as "uh-huh" and "yeah." Such expressions make the speaker sound dull, indifferent and uninterested.

Unit 6

Business Center

Objectives

- Memorize the specialized terms and expressions.
- Understand the working procedures for various services in the business center.
- Offer services in a proper manner.

Lead-in

Match the pictures with the words given below.

A. fax machine   B. file folder   C. stapler

D. printer   E. computer   F. tariff

(1) _____

(2) _____

(3) _____

(4) _____

(5) _____

(6) _____

Part I Background Knowledge

Job Description for Business Center

The business center is specifically designed to aid the hotel's business clients, so that they may conduct their business affairs during their stay. The business center staff will need to be able to perform secretarial services such as typing, printing, faxing, and photocopying materials for guests. A skilled business center operative should possess strong computer skills, be technologically savvy, and be trained in using numerous devices of advanced office equipment. Besides, patience, carefulness and enthusiasm are still the principles to be followed by the personnel working in the business center. Superior service and advanced facilities will make guests feel pleasant and convenient and make the hotel become their impressive memory.

Part II Situational Dialogues

Dialogue 1 Sending a Fax

Scene: Helen (H) is a clerk of the Business Center of Wuxi Intercontinental Hotel. She is serving a request from a guest named Brown (B).

H: Good morning, sir. What can I do for you?

B: Good morning. I'd like to send a fax back to my country.

H: Is that to Swiss, Mr. Brown?

B: Absolutely right. What's the rate for a fax to Swiss?

H: It is 5 US dollars per minute, service charge included.

B: That's reasonable.

H: And if the fax goes through but not clear, we waive the service charge but you still must pay the fee for the telephone line.

B: Even if the fax can't be read?

H: I'm afraid so.

B: Can I know the reason?

H: Because the Telephone Bureau charges us for the use of the line even if the quality of the fax is poor.

B: I see.

H: May I have the fax number, please?

B: Here you are.

H: Please sit down and wait for a second. I'll fax it right now. It will be done very quickly.

H: I'm sorry; the line is busy. I'll try again. Oh, there is an error report.

B: What seems to be the problem?

H: I'm not sure. There are a few possibilities. The other side may be out of paper, or maybe they don't have their fax machines hooked up to their phone. Would you like them to check on it?

B: Well, I would like to make a call to them.

(After that, Helen tries again.)

H: OK. It goes through this time.

Dialogue 2   Typing Documents for the Guest

Scene: Helen (H) is the clerk of the Business Center of Wuxi Intercontinental Hotel. A hotel guest, Mr. John Williams (W), comes in and asks her to type some documents.

H: Good morning, sir. How may I help you?

W: I have some important files to be typed.

H: Sure. How many pages please?

W: Almost 10.

H: Is the whole document in English?

W: Yes. Could you tell me the rate of typing?

H: For typing in English, we charge RMB 100 yuan per page, including the printing rate. Do you need us to print them out, sir?

W: Yes, of course.

H: Here's the sample of our fonts. Which do you prefer?

W: This one, please.

H: Yes. Ten pages in all. When do you expect to get them, sir?

W: Can you make it done before 6:00 p.m.?

H: Sure. It will be ready before 6:00 p.m.

W: Thank you. I really appreciate your efforts.

H: May I have your name and room number, sir? After we have finished the first draft, we'll ring you to check it and make necessary corrections. After that, we'll print the final draft.

W: OK. My name is John Williams, and my room number is 3268.

H: OK. Mr. Williams. See you later.

W: See you.

Dialogue 3   Photocopying Service

Scene: Ms. Ben White (W) comes to the business center. She asks the clerk, Helen (H), to photocopy some documents for her.

H: Good afternoon, Miss. What can I do for you?

W: Good afternoon. Can you have some files photocopied for me?

H: Well, the original one is not very clear, Miss. I'm afraid the copy will not be very good.

W: Just try one page and let me see.

H: OK. How about this one, Miss?

W: Well, can we try a little darker?

H: Sure. I'll try again. How about this time?

W: Good, that's a little better. By the way, can you reduce it?

H: No problem. How small would you like it, please?

W: Half the size.

H: I see. Now you can find that this comes out quite well.

W: That's it.

H: How many copies do you want, Miss?

W: 15 copies, please.

H: Would you like me to staple them?

W: Yes, please. What's the charge?

H: 20 yuan, Miss. How would you like to pay?

W: I'll sign the bill.

H: Thank you, Miss. Please show me your room card and sign your name here.

W: No problem.

H: Thank you, Miss White. Here is the receipt. Please keep it. Have a good day!

Dialogue 4   Postal Service

Scene: Helen Jones (H), a guest in Wuxi Intercontinental Hotel, wants to mail something to the UK. Lily (L), the clerk of the hotel, is receiving her.

L: Good morning, Miss. May I help you?

H: Good morning. Can you mail this parcel for me?

L: Certainly, Miss. Would you like it to go by ordinary air mail or by express?

H: By express, please. It's urgent.

L: OK, by express.

H: By the way, Christmas is drawing near. I'd like to send several letters and Christmas cards to my family and friends at home.

L: Sure. How would you like to send them, by air or by surface mail?

H: How long does it take to go by surface mail?

L: Around half a month.

H: Oh, it's too long. How long does it take by air?

L: Maybe a week, Miss.

H: I prefer it by air. I really hope my family and friends can receive them before Christmas.

H: Thank you. What is the total postage?

L: Let me check ... The total postage is RMB 210 yuan, please.

H: OK. Here is the money for the postage.

L: Thank you, Miss. Here are your change and the receipt. Have a good day!

Part Ⅲ　Useful Expressions

1. React if you can't hear well the guest's saying.

Could you speak more slowly, please?

Could you kindly repeat it for me, please?

Could you speak a little louder?

Sorry, I didn't catch you.

Sorry, I didn't get what you said. I can't hear you very well.

I can barely hear you.

I'm having trouble hearing you.

Would you explain more for me?

2. Help guests with Internet service.

The Internet is free for our hotel guests.

You can open the Internet Explorer at first, and then you will come to the homepage of our hotel and get two choices—"Accept" and "Deny". Please click "Accept" and then your laptop will be connected to the Internet.

Sorry. May I ask our butler to go to your room and help you set up Internet connectivity?

3. Help guests send a fax.

Where do you want to fax?

Faxing will be charged on time.

May I have the fax number, please?

There is an error report on it.

I'll fax it right now.

4. Help guests with mails.

Would you want it to go by ordinary air mail or by express?

How would you like to send them?

The total postage is RMB 210 yuan, please.

Do you wish to send them by EMS (Express Mail Service)?

5. Help guests with photocopies.

Would you like me to try again?

Do you want to try it a little darker?

Can I do it a little lighter?

It will be clearer if we reduce it smaller.

Part Ⅳ　Activities

1. Vocabulary: Get the correct meanings and learn them by heart.

Words and Expressions	Meanings	Words and Expressions	Meanings
Business Center		facility	
secretarial		postal	
type		parcel	
print		facsimile machine	
fax		software	
photocopy		hook up	
device		sample of font	
office equipment		postage	
enthusiasm		EMS	
receipt		surface mail	

2. Role-play.

Situation 1: John Brown comes to the business center. He wants to mail a parcel and some postcards to his home country. You are the clerk in business center. Please help John.

Situation 2: John Brown comes to the business center and wants to have some documents typed and printed. Please help him to have these done.

3. Practical writing.

Retention Letter used in Hotels

Retention is charged for a reservation if a guaranteed reservation has been cancelled or had become a No Show. No matter how thorough or attentive the reservation agent had taken the reservation process there is no way to avoid an occasional reservation amendment or cancellation. Thus, retention letters or cancellation letters are often used in hotels to inform guests hotel policies for these occasions. Here is a sample for you.

Hotel Name

Address,

T ＋99-999-9999999, F ＋99-999-9999999

E: admin@ABChotel.com, W: www.abchotel.com

Dear (Guest Name),

Thank you for choosing (Hotel Name) to make a reservation for (Guest name) guest！This is with reference to your conversation with/email to (Reservation agent name) regarding the amendment/cancellation/no-show/early check-out of（Guest Name）at （Hotel Name）from date to date. As detailed in the confirmation sent to you earlier, a retention charge will be levied, as this change was made after the cut-off date. The policy as sent to you in your reservation confirmation mail.

Cancellation/amendment and no-show policy

- To guarantee your reservation, please provide the hotel with your credit card number and the card expiry date. Confirmation for the reservation would only be given on the basis of a valid credit card.

- In case there is any no-show or a cancellation/amendment (in part or full), within 72 hours or less from the date of check-in, a retention charge, of 1 night's applicable room rate, will be levied. In addition, should the guest check-out early, 1 night's retention will be charged in lieu of the night(s) being released.

We will be debiting the credit card provided at the time of the reservation for an amount of Rs plus applicable taxes i.e. 1 night's room rate.

Thanks and Regards,

（Reservation Agent）

Part V Further Reading

Global Code of Ethics for Tourism

As a fundamental frame of reference for responsible and sustainable tourism, the **Global Code of Ethics for Tourism** (GCET) is a comprehensive set of principles designed to guide key-players in tourism development. Addressed to governments, the travel industry, communities and tourists alike, it aims to help maximise the sector's benefits while minimizing its potentially negative impact on the environment, cultural heritage and societies across the globe.

Adopted in 1999 by the General Assembly of the World Tourism Organization, its acknowledgement by the United Nations two years later expressly encouraged UNWTO to promote the effective follow-up of its provisions. Although not legally binding, the Code features a **voluntary implementation mechanism** through its recognition of the role of the **World Committee on Tourism Ethics** (WCTE), to which stakeholders may refer matters concerning the application and interpretation of the document. Its Code's **10 articles** amply cover the economic, social, cultural and environmental components of travel and tourism.

Unit 7
Cashier Service

Objectives

- Use the specialized terms and expressions for cashier service.
- Understand the working procedures of exchanging foreign currencies.
- Master how to check out guests.

Lead-in

1. Match the pictures with the words given below.

A. passport   B. room card   C. credit card

(1) _____

(2) _____

(3) _____

2. Match the following currencies with its countries and regions in the form below.

A. Renminbi   B. Macao Pataca

C. HongKong Dollar   D. Won

E. Singapore Dollar   F. Japanese Yen

G. Thai Baht   H. Indian Rupee

I. Australian Dollar   J. South African Rand

K. Euro   L. Russian Ruble

M. Egyptian Pound   N. Canadian Dollar

O. U.S.Dollar   P. Pound Sterling

Q. New Zealand Dollar

序号	国家/地区	货币名称		货币符号	
		中文	英文	原有旧符号	标准符号
1	中国	人民币元		RMB¥	CNY
2	中国澳门	澳门元		PAT.；P.	MOP
3	中国香港	港元		HK $	HKD
4	韩国	韩元		₩	KRW
5	日本	日元		¥；J.¥	JPY
6	新加坡	新加坡元		S. $	SGD
7	泰国	泰铢		BT.；Tc.	THB
8	印度	卢比		Re.复数：Rs.	INR
9	澳大利亚	澳大利亚元		$ A.	AUD
10	新西兰	新西兰元		$ NZ.	NZD
11	欧洲货币联盟	欧元		EUR	EUR
12	俄罗斯	卢布		Rbs.Rbl.	RUB
13	英国	英镑		£；£Stg.	GBP
14	加拿大	加元		Can. $	CAD
15	美国	美元		U.S. $	USD
16	埃及	埃及镑		£E.；LF.	EGP
17	南非	兰特		R.	ZAR

Part I Background Knowledge

Job Description for Front Office Cashier

For a cashier, he or she will post revenue center charges to guest accounts, receive payments from guest accounts at check-out, and coordinate the billing of credit card and direct-billed guest accounts with the accounting division. All guest accounts are balanced by the cashier at the close of each shift. He/She normally entails answering guest inquiries regarding fees and services.

Foreign currency exchange and traveler's cheque exchange is a facility offered to their guests by the hotel. Usually, hotels have a tie-up with authorized currency exchange dealers. Front desk staff should follow the SOP for foreign currency exchange while handling currency exchange requests from the guest. These dealers send currency exchange rates to the hotel on a daily basis, which is updated on their software and also displayed on the cashier desk.

Part Ⅱ   Situational Dialogues

Dialogue 1   Pay the Bill in Cash

Scene: Mr. Williams (W) comes to the front desk to check out. Helen (H) receives him. Williams pays the bill in cash.

H: Good morning, sir. Can I help you?

W: Morning. I'd like to settle my bill.

H: Certainly, sir. Which room did you stay, please?

W: Room 2021.

H: Did you use any hotel services this morning?

W: No.

H: Please wait for a minute, sir. I'll print your bill.

W: Thank you.

H: Here you are, Mr. Williams. Please check it. Could you just sign here, please? How are you going to pay, in cash, by credit card or with traveler's checks?

W: In cash, please.

H: The total is RMB 1540 yuan, including the service charge.

W: Here you are.

H: Thank you. Here is your receipt and your change, Mr. Williams. Your change is RMB 60 Yuan.

W: Thank you very much.

H: You are welcome. Goodbye.

Dialogue 2   Pay the Bill with Traveler's Checks

Scene: Williams (W) comes to the front desk to check out. Helen (H) is receiving him. Williams pays the bill with traveler's checks.

H: Good afternoon, sir. What can I do for you?

W: Yes. I want to check out.

H: Could I have your name and room number, please?

W: My name is John Williams, from Room 3256. I called reception about an hour ago and asked them to prepare it. I have to leave soon.

H: Just a moment, please. Mr. Williams, did you have any charges for this morning? And have you used any hotel services since breakfast?

W: Yes, I used the mini-bar. I drank a bottle of juice.

H: All right. Here is the bill, sir. Please check it.

W: OK. Let me see. Yeah, that's right. Can I pay with traveler's checks?

H: Certainly, sir.

W：All right. Here you are.

H：Mr. Williams, could you please sign your name here?

W：All right.

H：Thank you and here is your receipt. Is your luggage packed in your room and is it ready?

W：Yes. It is ready.

H：I will call the Bell Captain to send it down for you.

W：Thank you very much.

H：You are welcome. Have a nice journey.

Dialogue 3　Pay the Bill by Credit Card

Scene：Williams（W）comes to the front desk to check out. Helen（H）is receiving him. Williams pays the bill by credit card.

W：Morning. I'd like to check out, please.

H：Good morning, sir. May I know your name and room number, please?

W：I'm John Williams. Room 2016. Here is the room card.

H：Thank you. Have you used the mini-bar or other services this morning?

W：I didn't use the mini-bar, or any other services.

H：OK. Mr. Williams. One moment, I'll get the bill ready for you. Your bill totals RMB 810 yuan. Here you are. Have a check, please.

W：Correct. But I don't have enough cash for it. May I pay by credit card?

H：Yes, we do accept some major credit cards. What card do you have?

W：Visa Card.

H：Fine. May I take an imprint of it?

W：Here it is.

H：Thank you. Just a moment. Please sign your name on the print, Mr. Williams.

W：OK. Here you are.

H：Thank you. Please take your credit card and keep the receipt. Have a nice journey.

H：Thank you very much. Goodbye.

Dialogue 4　Explain the Bill to the Guest

Scene：Williams（W）comes to the front desk to check out. Helen（H）is receiving him and explains some numbers on the bill.

H：Good morning, sir. May I help you?

W：I'd like to check out, please.

H：May I have your room number, please?

W：It is 2358. Here is the room card.

H：Mr. Williams, wait a minute please while I print the bill for you.

W：That's all right.

H: Here is your bill; please check it, Mr. Williams.

W: Oh, the rate was RMB 520 yuan per night. What's this RMB 30 yuan for?

H: It is service charge for your dinner.

W: Oh, there might be something wrong with the bill here.

H: Oh, yes?

W: The bill shows that there is RMB 50 yuan for the minibar. But I have never used the minibar since I checked in.

H: I'm terribly sorry. This must be a mistake. I'll connect the Housekeeping and check it for you again.

(A moment later ...)

H: I'm awfully sorry. It seems there is a mistake from the Housekeeping. I'll correct it right now.

W: That's all right.

H: Now let me give you another bill and please check it. Here is the money you overpaid.

W: Thank you.

C: I'm awfully sorry to have caused you so much trouble. We will try to be more careful in the future.

Dialogue 5 Foreign Currency Exchange

Scene: Williams (W) comes to the front desk to change money into RMB. Helen (H) is receiving him.

H: Good afternoon, sir. Can I help you?

W: I'd like to change some US dollars and I'd like to know today's exchange rate.

H: According to today's exchange rate, one US dollar in cash is equivalent to RMB 6.8 yuan. How much would you like to change, sir?

W: Well, I'll change one hundred and here's the money.

H: Please fill in this exchange memo, your passport number and the total sum, and sign your name here.

W: All right.

H: Thank you. You'll have it right away.

W: OK. Will you please give me some one-yuan notes? I need some small change.

H: All right. (... changing the money ...)

H: Mr. Williams, here it is. Please have a check and keep the exchange memo. You can go to the Bank of China or the airport exchange office to change the left money back into dollars by showing the memo.

W: Oh, yes, you are so kind. Thanks a lot.

H: You are welcome.

Part III   Useful Expressions

1. Confirm the check-out details.

Are you going to check out now?

So you arrived in on Oct. 3rd, and the departure date is Oct. 6th. Am I correct?

You want to settle the bill now?

2. Make an apology to a guest.

I must apologize for the inconvenience.

Please accept my apologies for our mistake.

I'm terribly sorry for overcharging you.

I should apologize for wasting your time.

There has been an error. I'll check it with the department concerned. Would you mind waiting for a minute?

3. Explain the bill to the guest.

Here is your bill. Please have a check.

It totals RMB 1500 yuan.

The total is RMB 1500 yuan.

The total amount is RMB 1500 yuan.

That's for the minibar you used in the morning.

4. Ask the guest the methods of payment.

How are you going to pay, sir?

How would you like to settle the bill, sir?

Will you pay in cash?

So you want to pay by credit card?

We do accept traveler's checks.

Here is your change and receipt.

5. Offer foreign currency exchange to the guest.

According to today's exchange rate, 100 US dollars is equivalent to RMB 680 yuan.

How much would you like to change, sir?

Please keep the receipt; you'll have to present it when you want to change your money back.

Would you like small or large bills?

6. Give the guest the receipt.

Here is your receipt. Please check it.

Keep the invoice, sir.

Please sign here.

We need your signature here.

Here is the money you overpaid.

Part Ⅳ   Activities

1. Vocabulary: Get the correct meanings and learn them by heart.

Words and Expressions	Meanings	Words and Expressions	Meanings
cashier		service charge	
payment		change	
foreign currency exchange		mini-bar	
bill		WeChat Payment	
Ali Pay		exchange rate	
settle the bill		equivalent	
credit card		exchange memo	
traveler's check		Apple Pay	

2. Role-play.

   Situation 1: John wants to check out and change some US dollars into Chinese RMB. He wants to know the current exchange rate and needs some small change. You are the cashier and help him with it.

   Situation 2: Williams comes to the cashier's desk and wants to pay his bill. He has already paid the advance deposit. So he will check out in cash.

3. Practical writing.

Hotel Invoice

   A well-made invoice in the form of Microsoft Word or Excel will make all the payments be given accurately to the customers while they are at the hotel. Here is an invoice sample. Please calculate the total amount and fill out the invoice.

ABC   Hotel
★★★★★

[Address]			
[City, ST ZIP]			
Fax/Phone:			
Email:		INVOICE #	DATE
		889	2022/4/8
BILL TO		Room No:	ResNo:

Continued

Guest Name:	564	12346
Company/Travel Agent	GST No:	564
Address		
City	Arrival Date	Arr Time:
Mobile/Email	2022/4/4	16:00
Billing Notes	Departure Date	Dep Time:
	2022/4/6	11:00
DESCRIPTION	QTY	UNIT PRICE	AMOUNT
Room Charge - 04/04/2022	1	1000.00	
GST - 12 %	1	120.00	
Laundry -05/04/2022	2	10.00	
Room charge - 05/04/2022	1	1000.00	
GST - 12 %	1	120.00	
			-
			-
Thank you for your business!		TOTAL	

Regardless of the billing instruction I agree to be held personally liable for payment of the total amount of this bill.

Cashier Signature:	Guest Signature:

Thanks for Choosing - (Your Hotel Name)

Part V Further Reading

Global Code of Ethics for Tourism
Article 1
Tourism's contribution to mutual
understanding and respect between peoples and societies

（1）The understanding and promotion of the ethical values common to humanity, with an attitude of tolerance and respect for the diversity of religious, philosophical and moral beliefs, are both the foundation and the consequence of responsible tourism; stakeholders in tourism development and tourists themselves should observe the social and cultural traditions and practices of all peoples, including those of minorities and indigenous people and to recognize their worth.

(2) Tourism activities should be conducted in harmony with the attributes and traditions of the host regions and countries and in respect for their laws, practices and customs.

(3) The host communities, on the one hand, and local professionals, on the other, should acquaint themselves with and respect the tourists who visit them and find out about their lifestyles, tastes and expectations; the education and training imparted to professionals contribute to a hospitable welcome.

(4) It is the task of the public authorities to provide protection for tourists and visitors and their belongings; they must pay particular attention to the safety of foreign tourists owing to the particular vulnerability they may have; they should facilitate the introduction of specific means of information, prevention, security, insurance and assistance consistent with their needs; any attacks, assaults, kidnappings or threats against tourists or workers in the tourism industry, as well as the wilful destruction of tourism facilities or of elements of cultural or natural heritage should be severely condemned and punished in accordance with their respective national laws.

(5) When travelling, tourists and visitors should not commit any criminal act or any act considered criminal by the laws of the country visited and abstain from any conduct felt to be offensive or injurious by the local populations, or likely to damage the local environment; they should refrain from all trafficking in illicit drugs, arms, antiques, protected species and products and substances that are dangerous or prohibited by national regulations.

(6) Tourists and visitors have the responsibility to acquaint themselves, even before their departure, with the characteristics of the countries they are preparing to visit; they must be aware of the health and security risks inherent in any travel outside their usual environment and behave in such a way as to minimize those risks.

Unit 8

Settling Guests' Complaints

Objectives

- Use the specialized terms and expressions for settling complaints.
- Understand the working procedures of settling guests' complaints.
- Master the skills for settling complaints.

Lead-in

1. Think it over and share your ideas with your classmates.

Hotel industry emphasizes more on soft skills, like communication and problem-solving abilities. Do you agree with it? Discuss with your partner, and list the soft skills that you think are important and then share with your classmates.

2. Match the pictures with the words given below.

A. corridor	B. elevator	C. air conditioning
D. chambermaid	E. repairman	F. manager
G. towel	H. water closet	I. toiletry items

(1) _____

(2) _____

(3) _____

(4) _____

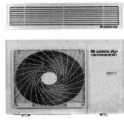
(5) _____

(6) _____

（7）＿＿＿＿

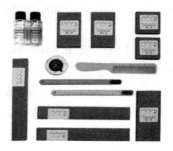
（8）＿＿＿＿

（9）＿＿＿＿

Part I　Background Knowledge

Top Ten Ways of Handling Guest Complaints

Listen with concern and empathy.

Isolate the guest if possible, so that other guests won't overhear.

Stay calm. Don't argue with the guest.

Be aware of the guest's self-esteem. Show a personal interest in the problem. Try to use the guest's name frequently.

Give the guest your undivided attention. Concentrate on the problem. DO NOT insult the guest.

Take notes. Write down the key facts to save time if someone else must get involved. Also, the guest tends to slow down when they see the front desk agent trying to write down the issue.

Tell the guest what can be done. Offer choices. Don't promise the impossible, and don't exceed your authority.

Set an approximate time for completion of corrective actions. Be specific, but do not underestimate the amount of time it will take to resolve the problem.

Monitor the progress of the corrective action.

Follow up. Even if the complaint was resolved by someone else, contact the guest to ensure that the problem was resolved satisfactorily.

Part II　Situational Dialogues

Dialogue 1　Handling Complaint about Slow Luggage Delivery

Scene: Helen (H) is the front desk clerk of Wuxi Intercontinental Hotel. She is receiving a call from a guest named Williams (W). He complains that his luggage has not been sent to his room in about one hour.

H: Good afternoon. Wuxi Intercontinental Hotel, front desk, Helen speaking, how can I help you?

W: Yes, I checked in one hour ago. But my luggage still has not been sent to my room yet. What is the problem?

H: I am awfully sorry, sir. May I have your name and room number?

W: Henry Williams, Room 5218.

H: I'll check it for you right now and could you tell me some features of your luggage?

W: Sure, there are three pieces, one big brown suitcase, one black briefcase and one rucksack in green.

H: Thank you. Mr. Williams, are there any name tags on them?

W: Yes, my name tags are attached on each of them.

H: Very good, Mr. Williams. I will contact the Bell Desk right now, and then send your luggage to your room as soon as possible.

W: That would be fine.

(The phone rings in Williams' room.)

H: Mr. Williams, this is the front desk. Helen speaking. And we have got your luggage and it will be sent to your room in 3 minutes.

W: Good, thank you.

H: Mr. Williams, I am sorry for the trouble we have brought you. A large meeting group is checking in now, so our bell desk is a little busy. I do hope you can understand.

W: I understand.

H: Thank you very much. Mr. Williams, if there is anything we can do for you, please don't hesitate to let us know.

W: Sure. See you.

H: Have a nice stay! Goodbye.

Dialogue 2　Handling Complaint about Poor Service at Front Desk

Scene: Henry Williams (W) is calling the front office of Wuxi Intercontinental Hotel to complain about poor service he received at the front desk. Helen (H), the duty manager answers the call.

H: Good morning, front office, Helen speaking, how can I help you?

W: Yes, of course. I want to speak to the hotel manager, please?

H: I am the duty manager, Helen. Is there anything I can do for you, sir?

W: My name is John Williams. I would like to file a complaint of the poor service of your hotel. This is my first time to stay here and it will be my last one too.

H: I am sorry to hear that. Could you tell me exactly what it is all about?

W: When I checked in yesterday, the two girls at the front desk were quite rude. They were chatting with each other. And when I asked about some information of the local sceneries, they just threw a pamphlet at the desk and went on their chatting. That is very unprofessional.

H: Mr. Williams, I do apologize for what happened. I will look into it and give you a reply as soon as possible.

W: Thank you for your attention in this matter. I really appreciate that.

H: Could you give me a number that I can reach you?

W: 138-525-567.

H: OK, Mr. Williams, thank you so much for calling us. I sincerely ask you to come back to our hotel again and I promise you that what happened to you yesterday will not repeat. Have a good day! Bye!

W: Bye.

Dialogue 3   Complaint about the Room

Scene: Mrs. Williams (W) comes to the front office with anger, and she complains that there are smells of cigarette in their nonsmoking room. Helen (H) tries to comfort her and help her to contact the manager (M) on duty to solve the problem.

H: Good evening, Miss. How may I help you?

W: Yes, we just checked in, but our room is unacceptable. It's Room 1810.

H: What is wrong with the room?

W: When we got into the room, there are strong smells of smoke. You see what we have reserved is absolutely a non-smoking room.

H: I'm sorry to hear that. Let me check. Yes, that room is supposed to be a non-smoking room. Well, somebody certainly didn't follow the rules.

W: The curtain smells like cigars. We can hardly breathe, and the windows won't open.

H: Right, the windows don't open, Miss. I'm really sorry about this. Let me see if I can find you another room.

W: Yes, please. We certainly can't stay in that room. Both of our kids have asthma, so the unclean air may cause breathing problems easily.

H: Yes, I understand your concern. Children can't stay in such a room. Please wait for a second. Oh, I'm afraid we don't have any other rooms with two double beds. If you excuse me, I'll speak with my manager. Sorry about this.

W: We are really tired, and we would like to get some rest as soon as possible.

H: Yes, I understand. If you don't mind, could you wait in the lounge near the elevators? It won't take long time.

W: Sure, I hope it will be done soon.

M: Good evening. I'm the manager here. I'm sorry to hear about your room.

H: Yes, we are not happy, and we are really tired. I hope you can help us.

M: I'm sure we can. Since we don't have another non-smoking room for you, I'll upgrade you to a suite. Would that be all right?

W: Yes, that would be fine. There is no extra cost, right?

M: Of course, there will be no extra charge.

W: And it's non-smoking, right?

M: I'm sure about that. I've confirmed that it's non-smoking.

W: Thanks. I really appreciate your help.

M: It's my pleasure. I hope you and your family have a wonderful stay with us. Here is my card. If there is anything else I can do for you, please let me know.

W: I will. Have a good evening.

M: Thank you, and once again, let me apologize again for the inconvenience we've brought you.

Dialogue 4　Complaint about Parking Fee

Scene: A hotel guest, Mr. Williams (W), complains that the hotel has charged him parking fees as he is a staying guest. The receptionist, Helen (H) explains that the parking space doesn't belong to the hotel and the fee charged is reasonable.

H: Good morning, may I help you?

W: I want to complain. I am staying in your hotel. Why do you charge me a parking fee? The other hotels I lived in Shanghai never charged me for parking. They are free.

H: I am sorry, sir. We don't have our own parking space, and this parking area belongs to International Gymnasium next to us. They charge whether you stay in our hotel or not. Actually, your parking should be charged 10 yuan per hour. 30 yuan for overnight parking is not too much, and they do have good security. I hope you can understand.

W: OK. Now I see.

Part Ⅲ　Useful Expressions

1. **Inquire problems of a guest with a complaint.**

    Excuse me, sir. Would you tell me what happened?

    What seems to be the problem, sir/madam?

    Could you give me details about it?

    Could you tell me exactly what it is about?

    Could I know what is wrong with your room?

2. **Apologize to the guest.**

    I'm terribly sorry you've been troubled.

    We do apologize for the inconvenience.

    I'm awfully sorry. It must have been a mistake.

3. **Show sincerity to the guest.**

    Thank you for bringing the matter to our attention.

    I assure you that it won't happen again.

    I do understand how you feel.

    We do the best to solve the problem.

    I promise you that what happened to you yesterday will not happen again.

4. Tell guests actions taken to solve the problem.

　　We have found your luggage. It is on the way to your room.

　　We offer you 10 percent discount for your room charge.

　　Shall I get the duty manager here, sir?

　　We will change another room for you now.

　　We update your room to a suite, no more charge for that.

Part Ⅳ　Activities

1. Vocabulary: Get the correct meanings and learn them by heart.

Words and Expressions	Meanings	Words and Expressions	Meanings
complaint		insult	
problem-solving ability		delivery	
feedback		name tag	
guest satisfaction		poor service	
potential guest		non-smoking room	
rucksack		parking fee	
asthma		reasonable	
security procedure		empathy	
duty manager		feature	
exceed		frequently	
authority		apologize	
concern		suite	

2. Role-play.

　　Situation 1: A guest named Brown calls the front desk to complain about the slow delivery of the luggage. The receptionist asks Mr. Brown to describe the luggage's features. After checking, the staff tells Mr. Brown that his stuff is on the way.

　　Situation 2: Mr. Brown comes to the duty manager and complains that he could not sleep well last night, because of the noises from the baggage elevator. You are the duty manager, and try to help him.

3. Practical writing.

Apology Letter Format to Hotel Guests

　　Guests staying at the hotel occasionally are disappointed or may find fault with services or facilities at the hotel. Hotel management should be attentive to guests with complaints and seek a timely and satisfactory resolution to the problem and also send a personalized apology letter to the guest via email/fax/mail as part of the service recovery process in the hotel. Here is a sample for you.

Letter of Apology

February 1st, 2022

Dear Mr. /Mrs. /Miss/Ms. (Guest Name),

Please allow me an opportunity to introduce myself; my name is (**Your Name**) and I am the general manager at the (**Hotel Name**), (**City Name**). My guest service team has advised me of the service you received during your stay with us; first and foremost I want to sincerely apologize for this.

We always strive to provide the best service to our guests and especially to regular guests such as you, but on this occasion we did not exceed your basic expectation.

I would like to extend an invitation to you and your family to stay with us the next time your travel (**Mention City Name**). Please be kind enough to contact me directly and I will personally ensure that you are VIPs. And I will extend a special discounted rate with complimentary breakfast to order.

I look forward to hearing from you and looking forward to welcoming you at (**Hotel Name**).

Yours sincerely,

General Manager

Part V Further Reading

Global Code of Ethics for Tourism
Article 2
Tourism as a vehicle for individual and collective fulfillment

(1) Tourism, the activity most frequently associated with rest and relaxation, sport and access to culture and nature, should be planned and practised as a privileged means of individual and collective fulfilment; when practised with a sufficiently open mind, it is an irreplaceable factor of self-education, mutual tolerance and for learning about the legitimate differences between peoples and cultures and their diversity.

(2) Tourism activities should respect the equality of men and women; they should promote human rights and, more particularly, the individual rights of the most vulnerable groups, notably children, the elderly, the handicapped, ethnic minorities and indigenous peoples.

(3) The exploitation of human beings in any form, particularly sexual, especially when applied to children, conflicts with the fundamental aims of tourism and is the negation of tourism; as such, in accordance with international law, it should be energetically combatted with the cooperation of all the States concerned and penalized without concession by the national legislation of both the countries visited and the countries of the

perpetrators of these acts, even when they are carried out abroad.

(4) Travel for purposes of religion, health, education and cultural or linguistic exchanges are particularly beneficial forms of tourism, which deserve encouragement;

(5) The introduction into curricula of education about the value of tourist exchanges, their economic, social and cultural benefits, and also their risks, should be encouraged.

Note: For Article 3 to 10, you may visit the website of UNWTO at www.unwto.org.

Chapter 2　Housekeeping Department

A Hotel Room of Crowne Plaza，Wuxi

As an important department in the operation of the hotel，the main task of the housekeeping is to provide guests with a comfortable，quiet，elegant and safe accommodation environment，and offer convenient，thoughtful and sincere service to guests according to their habits，characteristics and requirements.

Unit 9

Guide Guests to Their Rooms

Objectives

- Escort guests to hotel rooms following working procedures.
- Introduce hotel facilities to the guests.
- Introduce room facilities to the guests.

Lead-in

1. Think it over and share your ideas with your classmates.

Do you know any theme rooms in the hotel, such as Hello Kitty rooms, panda rooms? Describe a theme room to your classmates with PPT, if possible.

2. Match the following pictures with the words given below.

A. socket   B. air conditioner switch   C. room card
D. housemaid   E. switch board   F. curtain

(1) _____

(2) _____

(3) _____

(4) _____

(5) _____

(6) _____

Part I Background Knowledge

Job Description of Accommodations Manager

Accommodations manager ensures that all guest bedrooms and public areas are cleaned according to the highest standard. He/She also directly manages the housekeeping department and oversees front office operations in the absence of front office manager, ensuring that the staff are in strict compliance with the hotels' policies and regulations.

Part II Situational Dialogues

Dialogue 1 Accompany Guests to Their Room

Scene: The Blacks come out of the elevator and try to find their room.

FA: the floor attendant   B: Mr. Black   M: Mrs. Black

FA: Good afternoon, sir and madam. Did you have a nice trip?

B: Yes, thanks.

FA: Welcome to the ninth floor. I'm the floor attendant. Please let me know if there is anything I can do for you.

B: Where is Room 908, please?

FA: Step this way, please, Mr. and Mrs. Black.

M: Oh, how do you know our names?

FA: It was on the arrival list for Room 908. Here we are. May I have your key, please? Let me open the door for you.

B: Here it is.

FA: (The floor attendant knocks at the door first, opens it, and precedes the guests into the room and turns on the light.) This way, please.

B: Thank you. When will our baggage arrive?

FA: Your suitcase will be here soon. The bellman is handling them.

B: Very well. (looking around the room)

FA: How do you like this room?

M: Oh, it looks comfortable and cozy. We like it very much.

FA: (drawing the curtains aside) The room is facing south and enjoys a good view of the Grand Canal.

M: Yes, how lovely it is!

FA: (handing the room key to Mr. Black) Here is your key, Mr. Black. Have a nice stay in our hotel. Goodbye!

B: Bye-bye.

Dialogue 2　Escort a Guest with Luggage to His Room

Scene: A clerk named Peter (P) is taking a guest to the room. The guest (G) has a lot of baggage.

P: Good afternoon, Mr. Wang. Welcome to our hotel.

G: Oh, how do you know my name?

P: The labels on your luggage.

G: You are so clever. This is the air consignment labels.

P: Thank you for your compliment, sir. I will show you to your room. Are there all your baggage?

G: Yes, could you give me a hand with the baggage?

P: Certainly, that's my responsibility.

G: Thank you.

P: Is there anything valuable or breakable in your bags?

G: Yes, there is a bottle of wine in this bag and that bag is full of books.

P: Sure, may I have a look at your room card, please?

G: Here you are.

P: Thank you. Your room is on the tenth floor, and please follow me. We will go up by the elevator.

G: OK.

P: This is your room. (unlocking the door and switching on light) After you, sir. Do you mind if I put your luggage by the wardrobe?

G: No.

P: If you need anything, just call the reception. The number is 9.

G: Thank you.

P: You are always welcome.

Dialogue 3　Introduce Hotel Facilities to the Guest

Scene: Ellen(E) has taken a guest into the room and the guest (G) wants to know the services and facilities in the room.

E: Please come in. This is the bathroom and the switch is here.

G: The room looks cozy and comfortable.

E: Thank you for your praise. Our restaurant serves breakfast from 7 a.m. to 10 a.m. Here is our brochure for you. You can find various services in our hotel.

G: Thank you. Could you tell me something about the restaurants in your hotel?

E: Sure. Here is a French Café and a Korean barbeque restaurant on the third floor. Also, we have a Chinese restaurant on the second floor.

G: Can I go shopping here?

E：Of course. There are a lot of nice shops and boutiques nearby.

G：Thank you.

E：You are welcome. We have both sauna and massage service in our hotel as well.

G：Good.　Here is something for you. (giving tips)

E：Thank you. Is there anything else I can do for you?

G：No，thank you.

E：Have a nice day！

Dialogue 4　Show the Amenities in the Room

Scene：The Floor Attendant（FA）is showing the Blacks（M & B）the amenities in the room.

FA：(graciously) Mr. and Mrs. Black，here are the light switches，the temperature adjuster，the wardrobe and the mini-bar. Here's our hotel's Service Information Booklet. It will give you an idea about our services and facilities.

M：Wonderful! Thank you.

FA：The panel on the night stands controls the different devices in the room. That door leads to the bathroom，and there're laundry bags in the wardrobe. The hot water supply is round the clock. And there're two sockets in the bathroom，for 110V and 220V respectively. The voltage here is much higher than that in the United States.

B：Oh，I can use my electronic shaver. And I feel like taking a bath to freshen up after the transoceanic flight.

FA：Is there anything else I can do for you before I leave the room?

M：You've made us feel very welcome. By the way，is the tap water drinkable?

FA：Oh，Mr. and Mrs. Black，please don't drink the tap water. There is boiled drinking water in the thermos bottle and cold drinking water in the carafe. If you need anything，please dial 8 or press the button over there.

B：Thank you very much.

FA：You're always welcome. I hope you will enjoy your stay with us.

Part Ⅲ　Useful Expressions

1. Escort guests to their rooms.

　　Please follow me.

　　May I have your room key，please?

　　Let me open the door for you.

　　May I put your baggage here?

　　Shall I draw the curtains for you?

　　The room has a view of the West Lake.

2. Show the amenities and facilities in the room to the guests.

　　Here is the wardrobe and there is the bathroom.

The switch is here.

Here is a brochure explaining the hotel service.

There are several kinds of drinks in the mini-bar. Please help yourself to them.

The cost of the drinks you've had in the min-bar will be added to your account.

Please insert the key card for electricity.

Please use the remote control for TV programs.

The electrical current in your room is 220 volts.

If you don't want to be disturbed, you'd better press the "Don't Disturb" key on the bedside controls.

Pull up the faucet valve, then turn it to the left and the heated water will run out.

I'll turn on /down /up /off the air-conditioning /heat for you. The temperature is a little bit low here. Let me adjust it to 20 degrees centigrade.

Part IV Activities

1. Vocabulary: Get the correct meanings and learn them by heart.

Words and Expressions	Meanings	Words and Expressions	Meanings
switch on		air-conditioning	
escort		cocktail	
consignment		compliment	
voltage		responsibility	
socket		valuable	
round the clock		drinkable	
amount to		tap water	
panel		brochure	
breakable		nightstand	
elevator		wardrobe	

2. Role-play.

Situation 1: A hotel staff member is showing a guest to his/her room. On the way, please introduce hotel facilities to the guest.

Situation 2: A guest with two suitcases is coming out of the elevator. Please help him/her find the room and introduce hotel services.

3. Translate the following sentences into Chinese.

(1) All our rooms are equipped with IDD system and DDD system.

(2) The extension number is exactly the same as your room number.

_____

(3) The room is facing south and commands a good view of the Huangpu River.

_____

(4) I'm the floor attendant. Just let me know if there is anything I can do for you.

_____

(5) The information booklet gives you an idea about our services and facilities.

_____

4. Read and learn.

Housekeeping Daily Routine Tasks Checklist

Room re-made and cleaned efficiently.

Allotted daily service completed by 6:00 p.m. (Timings depend upon hotel type)

No items should be removed from the guest room unless placed in the trash basket.

All flooring is swept/vacuumed.

Mirrors/pictures are free from dust and smudges.

Lamps, bulbs, shades and switches are free from dust, hair, streaks and fingerprints.

All bulbs, TV, hair dryer, Ipad/Ipod/mobile docking station are functional.

Beds are tightly and neatly made.

Guest money, jewellery, mobiles, laptops, valuables and personal items left untouched.

Newspapers and magazines are stacked and left in plain view.

Guest clothing found on the bed or floor are folded and placed on bed or chair; clothing left on furniture is folded and left in place.

Shoes are paired and placed to the side.

Laundry bag and order form are replaced and neatly presented.

All trash cans are emptied.

Sink, counter and mirror are wiped clean and spotless.

Tub and shower cleaned, no debris, dust, spots, stains or hair.

Toilet cleaned, no debris, dust, spots, stains or hair.

Used linen is removed and replaced.

Bathroom paper supplies are restocked and tissues are repointed.

Glasses are washed or replaced; coffee machine is set up, cleaned and restocked.

All interior windows and window sills are free of dust, hair, streaks and fingerprints.

Appropriate lighting is left on and TV channel reset to welcome screen.

Part V Further Reading

Impressive Themed Hotel Rooms That You Can't Resist Booking(1)

Some hotels are outdated and boring, but others have transformed their suites into special, jaw-dropping themed experiences. Travelers are spending the night in some creative rooms with stunning decorations inspired by popular films and books.

Here are impressive themed hotel rooms that you can't resist booking. These rooms will make you say, "Take my money!"

The Lisa Frank Flat │ Los Angeles，CA

Thanks to Hotels.com，'90s kids got the chance to relive their childhoods in an insane Lisa Frank-themed hotel suite(图 9-1). The suite is a rainbow dream, with unicorns, dolphins and cheetahs popping up everywhere. The bed has a light-up cloud canopy, and each wall is covered in technicolor murals. When guests go into the bathroom, they are transported into an underwater world. Sea creatures swimming in a blue and pink ocean are painted on the walls.

图 9-1　A Corner of the Lisa Frank Flat

There is also a large supply of neon gel pens, stickers and '90s lunch box snacks like Cheez Balls. Plus, guests won't go home empty-handed. The experience comes with limited-edition gifts, such as Lisa Frank-themed slippers, sleep masks and robes.

Room Cleaning Service

Objectives

- Offer cleaning service in guest rooms.
- Do turn-down service efficiently.
- Deal with situations concerned with room-cleaning.

Lead-in

1. Discuss with your classmates about what turn-down service is.

Here is some reference for you:

Turn-down service includes: making the bed; drawing the curtains; turning on some lights; cleaning the bathroom; taking away the rubbish; offering some hot water and so on.

2. Match the following pictures with the words given below.

A. bathroom   B. housemaid   C. wardrobe

D. wash basin   E. hair dryer   F. towel

(1) _____

(2) _____

(3) _____

(4) _____

(5) _____

(6) _____

Part I　Background Knowledge

Job Description of Assistant Executive Housekeeper

The assistant Executive Housekeeper supervises and coordinates activities of room attendants, house attendants, public area cleaners and floor supervisors. He/She assists in managing and directing the day-to-day operations of all housekeeping and laundry functions.

Part II　Situational Dialogues

Dialogue 1　Clean the Room While the Guest Is In

Scene: Diane (D) works in housekeeping. She comes to clean Mr. Pryor's (P) room.

D: Housekeeping. May I come in?

P: Come in, please.

D: Good morning, Mr. Pryor. I'm sorry to disturb you. Do you want me to come back later?

P: No. Please don't go. The room really needs cleaning.

D: OK, Mr. Pryor. I will clean your room.

P: Do you mind if I stay?

D: Not at all. The vacuum cleaner may be a little noisy. Is that OK?

P: No problem. Thank you.

D: I'll finish as quickly as I can.

P: Thank you. And could I get some extra towels, please?

D: Certainly. Small towels or big towels?

P: Big bath towels. It's so hot these days. I took two showers yesterday.

D: Yes. Is this trash, Mr. Pryor?

P: The newspaper is. Let me have a look at those papers.

D: Here you are.

P: Yes. This is all trash.

D: (after finishing cleaning the room) The bed is made and I put two extra towels in the bathroom.

P: Oh, great. Thank you.

D: You are welcome. Goodbye.

Dialogue 2　Turn-down Service

Scene: The housemaid (H) is offering the guest (G) turn-down service.

H: Good evening. May I do the turn-down service for you?

G: OK. And could I have an extra bed?

H: Yes, of course. But please call the reception desk first. I'll get you one with their permission.

G: How much does an extra bed cost?

H: Ten dollars per night.

G: OK. I'll call them then.

H: Would you like me to draw the curtains, madam?

G: That's nice. And turn on the lights, please.

H: Yes. Is there anything else I can do for you?

G: No more. Thank you.

H: You're welcome.

Dialogue 3   Clean the Room Improperly

Scene: The guest (G) is complaining to the receptionist (R) that the room is not cleaned properly.

R: Good morning, front desk. May I help you?

G: I'm afraid that housekeeping did not clean my room properly.

R: I'm terribly sorry, sir. What seems to be the problem?

G: There is dust on the coffee table and dresser. The mirror in the bathroom is full of water spots.

R: Please accept my apology on behalf of the hotel. I will send a room attendant to your room at once.

G: There is another problem. I don't think the pillowcases have been changed for three days.

R: I'll report the matter to the housekeeping supervisor. We will make sure this will not happen again.

G: Thank you.

R: Please don't hesitate to contact us again if you have any further problems.

G: OK.

Part III   Useful Expressions

1. Room cleaning.

When would you like me to make up your room, sir?

Would you like me to clean up your room right now, sir?

We'll come and clean your room immediately.

2. Turn-down service.

May I do the turn-down service for you now, sir/madam?

Shall I come back later?

Shall I draw the curtains for you, sir/madam?

May I turn on the lights for you?

Can I make the beds for you now or do you wish it to be done later?

Part IV Activities

1. Practice: Fill in the blanks with the words given below.

else	kind	Housekeeping	tidy	welcome	bathroom

A: __1__ , may I come in?

B: Come in, please.

A: Good evening, madam. May I __2__ your room now?

B: Sure. Could you tidy the __3__ first? I took a bath just now, and it's quite a mess.

A: Certainly, madam. Is there anything __4__ I can do for you?

B: Oh, yes, where can I borrow a hairdryer?

A: I'll send one up at once.

B: Thank you. You are so __5__ .

A: You are __6__ . Good night, madam. Have a nice dream.

2. Vocabulary: Get the correct meanings and learn them by heart.

Words and Expressions	Meanings	Words and Expressions	Meanings
turn-down service		towel	
vacuum		hair dryer	
dust		mattress	
polish		carpet	
wipe		wardrobe	
wash basin		empty the garbage	
change the sheets		trash can	
make the bed		blanket	
wastebasket (USA)		washcloth	
rubbish bin (UK)		duvet	
pillow		pillow case	

3. Role-play.

Situation 1: Lucy is a housekeeper. She wants to clean the room for Mrs. Smith. Mrs. Smith talks with Lucy while she is tidying the room. And Mrs. Smith wants some green tea and more drinkable water.

Situation 2: Miss Smith calls the reception desk for turn-down service. Please answer the phone politely and send a housemaid for her.

4. Read and learn.

Guest Bedroom Cleanliness and Service Standard

All flooring is free of dirt and debris including edges.

Carpet/Wooden flooring is in excellent repair and not worn or damaged.

Counter tops, furnishings, chairs and tables free of spots, dust, stains and marks.

All furnishings and upholstery are in sturdy condition and also free of wear and defects.

Ledges and baseboards are in good condition and free of dust and scuffs.

Lamp fixtures, decorative objects are free of dust.

Ceiling is in good condition, free of dust, cobwebs and stains.

All paintwork or wallpaper is in excellent condition, free of scuffs and marks.

Drawers inside are free of dust and debris, with ample space to open and close smoothly.

All waste bins are empty and in good condition.

Ashtrays, if present, are undamaged and also free of dirt and ashes.

Window/sliding glass are undamaged and free from smudges inside.

Picture frame glass is free of spots and dust on frames.

All mirror glass is undamaged, free of streaks and dust on frame.

TV/LCD/LED screen is free of streaks/spots, and all wires and cords are orderly hidden behind the screen.

All draw cords or handles to close curtains work easily.

Curtains are closed completely and provide complete blackout.

Beds are tightly and neatly made.

Mattress and box springs are aligned.

Bedspread and skirting are in good condition, not worn, free of stains, hair and debris.

Blankets are in good condition, not worn or damaged, free of stains, hair and debris.

Bed sheets are in good condition, not worn or damaged, free of stains, hair and debris.

Pillow cases are in good condition, not worn or damaged, free of stains, hair and debris.

Bed frame and headboard are in good condition, free of damage, dust and markings.

Wardrobe is in good condition, free of wear and damage, neatly arranged, and free of dust.

Sufficient supplies are provided (shoe shine, shoe polish, laundry bags, lists, etc.)

Hangers are matched and of good quality. And hangers consist of suit, padded and clip hangers (minimum of 8 to 10 hangers present).

In-room safe is not worn and works properly, and its instructions are easily understood.

Part V　Further Reading

Impressive Themed Hotel Rooms That You Can't Resist Booking(2)
Guest Rooms of InterContinental Shanghai Wonderland

InterContinental Shanghai Wonderland(图 10-1) is a luxury hotel located in Songjiang, Shanghai. It sits at 88 meters closer to the heart of earth. The hotel is an awe-inspiring destination bringing together affluent travelers to experience the glamour of InterContinental life in business, leisure and adventure travel.

图 10-1　InterContinental Shanghai Wonderland

There are 336 rooms and suites in the hotel. The interior style is inspired by cliffs, waterfalls and hills, presenting a visual feast with modern beauty. All rooms above the water level are provided with viewing terraces. There is an underwater suite on the B15 floor(图 10-2). Guests will be attracted by the swimming fish of aquarium. Up the stairs is the bedroom. The underwater view downstairs and the pit view upstairs are unique in the world.

图 10-2　Guest rooms of InterContinental Shanghai Wonderland

Unit 11

Laundry Service

Objectives

- Remember specialized terms and expressions for laundry service.
- Understand the working procedures of laundry service.
- Offer laundry services efficiently.

Lead-in

1. Match each of the English expressions with its Chinese version.

1. dry clean	A. 干洗
2. iron	B. 手洗
3. hand wash	C. 上浆
4. shrink	D. 缝补
5. sew	E. 不褪色的
6. colorfast	F. 褪色
7. starch	G. 熨烫
8. fade	H. 缩水

2. Match the pictures with the words given below.

A. trousers	B. T-shirt	C. shorts
D. sweater	E. jacket	F. dress
G. scarf	H. handbag	I. pajamas

(1) _____   (2) _____   (3) _____

(4) _____   (5) _____   (6) _____

(7) _____   (8) _____   (9) _____

Part Ⅰ Background Knowledge

The hotel has an in-house laundry facility and is pleased to supply this service daily. Laundry bags are located in the wardrobe ofthe room. When guests fill out the laundry form, hotel staff will pick up the laundry from guest rooms.

Types of the Laundry Service

Classified by the way of washing:

(1) Dry-cleaning   (2) Washing   (3) Pressing

Classified by the time of washing:

(1) Same day service: Send the laundry after 10/11 a.m. in the morning and get it back in the evening/around 6 p.m.;

(2) Express service: No more than 4 hours, but the guests have to pay extra charge for it. (Usually there is a 50 % extra charge for this service).

Part Ⅱ Situational Dialogues

Dialogue 1 Introduce Laundry Service

Scene: A Guest (G) is calling for laundry service. A clerk (C) is answering the phone and making personnel transfers as required.

G: Could you send someone up for my laundry?

C: Yes, sir. May I have your room number?

G: Room 1211.

C：OK，a laundry person will be there in a few minutes.

(three minutes later)

C：Laundry service. May I come in?

G：Come in，please. My suits need dry cleaning. Can I have them today?

C：Certainly，we have an express service. But we charge 50 percent more.

G：I see. I'll have the express service.

Dialogue 2　Fill out the Laundry Form

Scene：A guest（G）is inquiring about some details about laundry matters and procedures. A room maid（M）is answering her questions.

M：Housekeeping，may I come in?

G：Yes. I'd like to have this laundry done，please?

M：Certainly，madam. Could you fill out the laundry form，please?

G：Where is it?

M：It's in the drawer of the writing desk.

G：Fine. May I use your pen?

M：Certainly，madam. Here you are.

G：Thanks. Oh，I don't want these shirts starched.

M：No starch. I understand，madam.

G：Yes，and I'd like this sweater washed by hand in cold water. It may shrink otherwise.

M：By hand in cold water. I understand.

G：When will it be ready?

M：We will deliver them tomorrow evening around 6：00 p.m.

G：Fine. Thanks a lot.

M：You are welcome.

Dialogue 3　The Laundry Fee

Scene：A guest（G）wants his laundry to be done. He is also caring about the receipt he needs to pay. An operator（O）is answering his questions.

O：This is the laundry service. Can I help you?

G：I have some clothes that need to be washed，a few pairs of socks and a sweatshirt.

O：Well，just put your staff in the laundry bag.

G：How soon can I have them back?

O：Usually in a day. If you give it in the morning，maybe you'll get it by evening.

G：How much is it?

O：The rate chart is contained in the stationery folder in your dresser's drawer.

G：Oh，I see. Well，would you please send someone to Room 808 to pick up some laundry for me?

O: Yes, sir. The clerk will be there in a few minutes.

G: Thank you.

O: You are welcome.

Part Ⅲ Useful Expressions

1. Introduce laundry service to the guests.

There is a laundry bag in your bathroom.

We have an express service. But we charge 50 percent more.

We also offer hand wash service.

Please complete the laundry list and put it together with your laundry.

Is it for normal service or express service?

We only do simple mending.

2. Tell guests laundry fee and time.

The last laundry collection from guests is at 6 pm.

Express service takes three hours.

There's an extra 50 ％ charge for express service.

What time should we pick up your laundry?

Part Ⅳ Activities

1. Translation practice.

(1) Could you fill out the laundry form, please?

_____

(2) I don't want these shirts starched.

_____

(3) Could you send someone up for my laundry, please?

_____

(4) 这件衣服需要手洗。

_____

(5) 快洗服务需要加收 50％的费用。

_____

2. Vocabulary: Get the correct meanings and learn them by heart.

Words and Expressions	Meanings	Words and Expressions	Meanings
laundry		shrink	
express		deliver	
starch		sweatshirt	
laundry bag		rate chart	
stationery folder		drawer	

3. Role-play.

Lily White wants to have her dress cleaned. Now she is making a phone call to housekeeping. Make a conversation with the information given below.

Name：Lily White

Room Number：1126

Service：express laundry

Clothes：silk dress

Time to Return：6 p.m. today

Reason：To attend a party at 8 p.m. today.

Special Request：dry clean

4. Read and learn.

A Sample of Hotel Information Sheet

Generally, hotel information sheet is kept on all guest rooms. This helps to give an overview of all services and facilities provided by the hotel to the guests.

And this sheet also contains the details and timing of in-house restaurants, Spa etc. along with the direct extension number for Reception, Housekeeping and Room Service.

Hotel General Information

Kindly contact the front desk team at extension "22", to get more details about the services listed below.

Drinking Water

Water from the tap is not potable. You will find two complimentary bottles of drinking water in your room daily. Additional supplies will be charged to your account.

Adaptor

Multi-pin adaptor and extension box is available upon request.

Extra Bed and Cribs

It is available upon request. There will be additional charge for extra bed.

Doctor on Call

Should you require medical attention, a nurse is on standby 24 hours a day at the hotel and a doctor is on call at all times for emergencies. Doctor's fee can be billed to your room account.

Safety Deposit Box

Guest are advised to use the hotel's safety deposit boxes located on all guest rooms for keeping their valuables as the hotel's liability is limited for such items. Safety boxes are also available at the front desk.

Executive Club Lounge

Located on the (mention floor), it is for the exclusive use of those staying in our premier and executive rooms. It's open from 6 a. m. to 10 p. m. Facilities include complimentary breakfast, evening cocktails with snacks, coffee and tea throughout the day.

Mini Bar

For your convenience and refreshment a selection of beverages and snacks are available in your room. The mini bar will be re-stocked on a daily basis and the consumption is billed to your room account. Should you have other requirements, please contact our staff.

Baby Sitting

We provide baby sitting services, but please note that enough notice time (minium 24 hrs) is required.

Shoeshine

A shoeshine cloth can be found in the wardrobe. Should you wish to have your shoes polished, please contact us. Do not put your shoes outside your room.

Fitness Center and Spa

Our fitness center and spa is located on the 25th floor. Exercise equipment, aerobic, sauna, traditional massage etc. are available. Please call extension "35" for more details.

Part V　Further Reading

Impressive Themed Hotel Rooms That You Can't Resist Booking(3)
V8 Hotel | Böblingen, Germany

Make a pit stop at the V8 Hotel(图 11-1), a motor-inspired destination full of automotive history and rooms themed around the car of your dreams. One room boasts British race cars, while another displays vehicles made in Germany.

图 11-1　A Room of V8 Hotel

V8 Hotel offers 34 rooms with various car themes, but the luxurious Mercedes Suite steals the show. Illustrations, photographs and original parts cover the suite. It also features four floors and a rooftop terrace. However, the most notable feature is the flashy Mercedes car bed.

Unit 12

Maintenance Service

Lead-in

Match the pictures with the words given below.

A. shower   B. air conditioner   C. lamp

D. water closet   E. water tap   F. air conditioning remote control

(1) _____

(2) _____

(3) _____

(4) _____

(5) _____

(6) _____

Part Ⅰ   Background Knowledge

The articles in guest rooms frequently used by guests：

curtain 窗帘	slippers 拖鞋	hanger 衣架子
pillow 枕头	quilt 被子	wardrobe 衣柜
drawer 抽屉	duvet 羽绒被	bed cover 床罩
bed sheet 床单	blanket 毯子	light bulb 灯泡
mattress 床垫	coffee maker 咖啡机	shampoo 洗发水
conditioner 护发素	iron 熨斗	shoe horn 鞋拔子
toothbrush 牙刷	ironing board 熨衣板	floor lamp 落地灯
table lamp 台灯	soap 香皂	adapter 插头
safety box 保险箱	bath robe 浴袍	hair dryer 吹风机

Part Ⅱ   Situational Dialogues

Dialogue 1   Maintenance Service

Scene：A guest(G) is unsatisfied with her room temperature and its sound insulation effect，and a clerk(C) is communicating with her.

C：Housekeeping，may I help you?

G：Yes，my room is very cold. There must be something wrong with the air-conditioner.

C：I'm sorry，ma'am. I'll inform the maintenance department right now. What's your room number?

G：804.

C：Room 804. We will send someone to repair it at once.

G：It seems that there's something wrong with the temperature control panel.

C：Yes，I'll tell them. Any other problems?

G：It's so noisy that it's hard for me to fall asleep.

C：OK .We'll have the maintenance department check it for you. They'll be right there.

G：Thank you.

Dialogue 2   I Need a Brighter Light

Scene：A guest (G) wants a brighter light in his room. He rang for services and a hotel staff (HS) is to communicate with him.

HS：Good evening. Did you ring for service? What can I do for you?

G：The light in the room is too dim. Please get me a brighter one.

HS：I will bring the replacement immediately.

(*a few minutes later*)

HS：Housekeeping，may I come in?

G：Come in, please.

HS：I have brought a brighter light for you. Do you mind if I move your things?

G：Of course not.

HS：It's all right now. You may try it.

G：That's good. Thank you so much.

HS：You are welcome. Good night.

G：Good night.

Dialogue 3 The Remote Control does not Work

Scene：A guest（G）reports that the remote control does not work. A hotel technician（T） comes to inspect the problem.

(*The technician knocks at the door.*)

T：Maintenance department. May I come in?

G：Come in, please.

T：I'm from the maintenance department. Did you call us?

G：Yes. The air conditioner is not working properly.

T：Let me see. What's the problem?

G：The remote control doesn't work. I turned on the air conditioner, but I can't adjust the temperature.

T：Let me have a look. I think the batteries should be changed. Let me replace them with new ones. Now, it's working.

G：That's good.

T：Is there anything else I can do for you?

G：No, thanks.

T：If you have any problems, just call us. Have a good night!

G：Good night.

Dialogue 4 Fix the Desk Lamp for the Guest

Scene：A guest（G）asks the maintenance staff（S）to fix the desk lamp and the water tap in his room.

G：There's something wrong with the desk lamp.

S：The light bulb should be changed. I'll replace it with a new one.

G：Could you also have a look at the bathroom? The water tap is dripping all the time.

S：I'll check and see what the problem is.

G：Could you replace it with a new one?

S：There's no need, sir. I tightened the valve and it's not dripping now.

G：Yesterday, I came back and there was no hot water.

S：I'm sorry about that, but the water pipe of our hotel has been under repair. Hot water is not available between 12:00 p.m. and 5:00 a.m. every day.

G: I see. Thank you.

S: Hope you like our hotel.

G: I enjoy staying here.

Part III Useful Expressions

1. Ask guests about the problems.

> What is the matter?
>
> The bulb has burned out.
>
> The toilet doesn't flush.
>
> What can we do for you?
>
> The air-conditioner doesn't work.

2. Deal with problems.

> I'm sorry, Sir. I'll inform the maintenance department at once.
>
> We'll have the maintenance department check it for you.
>
> We'll send someone up to your room right away.
>
> Maintenance can be there in the next 15 minute.
>
> The water tap is dripping all the time.
>
> It needs to be replaced.
>
> Let me have a look. I will have it repaired.

Part IV Activities

1. Vocabulary: Get the correct meanings and learn them by heart.

Words and Expressions	Meanings	Words and Expressions	Meanings
maintenance		lamp	
technician		drip	
adjust		dim	
battery		light bulb	
replace		valve	
tighten		repair	

2. Role-play.

A guest is calling the front desk staff because there is something wrong with the toilet in his/her room. A repairman has to deal with this problem.

Here are some useful sentences for you.

What is your room number?

Room Maintenance, may I come in?

What's the trouble with the toilet?

Let me see; the toilet is clogged.

I will fix it for you.

Would you mind changing a room? The toilet is hard to repair today.

Sorry for the inconvenience. We do hope you enjoy your stay here.

3. Translation practice.

(1) 如果您需要其他东西，请与我们联系。

---

(2) The water tap drips all night long. I can hardly sleep.

---

(3) I am very sorry about the noise, sir. We will check into it.

---

(4) 怎么了，先生？

---

(5) 卫生间出什么毛病了？

---

(6) Is there anything to be repaired?

---

(7) We will send someone up to repair it.

---

(8) I am sorry, but we can't fix it today.

---

(9) Wait a moment, please. I will inform the Engineering Department to send someone to repair it.

---

(10) There is something wrong with the shower.

---

4. Read and learn.

Sample of Hotel Rules and Regulations

Hotel rules are management policies or agreements between the guest and the hotel. Usually, these policies are mentioned on the guest registration card which is signed by the guest at the time of check-in.

In addition to this, a copy of rules and regulations is also kept in all guest rooms for guests to read and understand the management policies. This can also include the local government policies which have to be followed by the guest.

Hotel Rules and Management Policies

In order to make your stay as pleasant as possible, the management requests your co-operation in observing the following as an agreement between the guest and the "Mention your Hotel Name here" (hereinafter called "Management") under which rooms are permitted to be used by the guest(s):

A. Tariff.

The tariff is for the room only and is exclusive of any government taxes applicable. Meals and other services are available at extra cost. To know your room tariff, please contact the Duty Manager. A guest registration form must be signed on arrival.

B. Settlement of bills.

Bills must be settled on presentation; personal cheques are not accepted.

C. Company's lien in guest's luggage and belongings.

In the case of default in the payment of dues by a guest, the management shall have the lien in their luggage and belongings, and be entitled to detain the same and to sell or auction such property at any time without reference to the guest. The net sale proceeds will be appropriate towards the amount due by the guest without prejudice to the management's rights to adopt such further recovery proceedings as may be required.

D. Check-in.

Please present your ID card, passport or temporary residence card upon check-in. By law visitors must present personal documents for hotel records. These documents will be returned upon departure.

E. Departure.

Check-out time is (**mention your checkout time here**). Please inform the reception if you wish to retain your room beyond this time. The extension will be given depending on the availability. If the room is available, the normal tariff will be charged. On failure of the guest to vacate the room on expiry or period, the management shall have the right to remove the guest and his/her belongings from the room occupied by the guest.

F. Luggage storage.

Subject to availability of the storage space, the guest can store luggage in the luggage room, at the guest's sole risk as to loss or damage from any cause. Luggage may not be stored for a period of over 30 days.

G. Guest's belongings.

Guests are particularly requested to lock the door of their rooms when going out or going to bed. For the convenience of the guest, electronic safety lockers are provided in the room to store any valuables.

The management will not in any way whatsoever be responsible for any loss or damage to the guest's belongings or any other property from either the hotel room or the locker or any other part of the hotel for any cause whatsoever including theft of pilferage.

H. Pets.

Mention your policy on pets (**allowed or not-allowed**)/(Allow us to make separate arrangements.)

I. Hazardous goods.

Bringing goods and/or storing of raw or exposed cinema or any other article of a combustible or hazardous nature and/or prohibited goods and/or goods of objectionable nature is prohibited.

The guest shall be solely liable and responsible to the management, its other guests, invitees, visitors, agents and servants for all loss financial or otherwise and damage that may be caused by such articles or as a result of the guests' own negligence and non-observance of any instructions.

Gambling, contraband, prostitution, weapons, explosives, flammable objects, poisons, drugs, animals and pungent food are strictly prohibited on hotel premises.

J. Damage to property.

The guest will be held responsible for any loss or damage to the hotel property caused by themselves, their guests or any person for whom they are responsible.

Part V Further Reading

Impressive Themed Hotel Rooms That You Can't Resist Booking(4)
Cave Room | Yucca Valley, CA

Check into a hidden gem in California's Joshua Tree National Park, Oasis of Eden. The themed cabin is owned by America's Best Value Inn, making it affordable for anyone who is interested. However, Oasis of Eden is not your average motel. This property provides one-of-a-kind experiences.

The motel offers 13 marvelous themed rooms, but the Cave Room(图 12-1) is the most unforgettable adventure. It comes with a spacious hot tub surrounded by stone and a round bed covered in leopard print. The decorations will make you feel like you're in a real cave.

图 12-1 The Cave Room

Unit 13

Room Service

Objectives

- Remember specialized terms and expressions for room service.
- Offer room service to the guests in a proper manner.
- Have a good knowledge of breakfast in different styles.

Lead-in

1. Discuss with your classmates:

Why do people ask for room service in the hotel? What do they want? What kind of service do you think they would prefer?

2. Match the following pictures with the words given below.

| A. sandwich | B. apple juice | C. coffee |
| D. plate | E. steak | F. milk |

(1) _____

(2) _____

(3) _____

(4) _____

(5) _____

(6) _____

Part I   Background Knowledge

Job Description of In-Room Dining Manager

An IRD Manager assists in management and administration and all operational aspects for the in room dining department. He/She also maintains the high quality of services.

He/she is expected to market ideas to promote business, reduce employee turnover; maintain revenue and payroll budgets; and meet budgeted productivity while keeping quality consistently high.

Part II   Situational Dialogues

Dialogue 1   Tell Guests How to Get Room Service

Scene: A guest (G) wants to take his breakfast in the room next morning; a clerk (C) is explaining room service to him.

G: I'd like to have breakfast in our room tomorrow morning. Could you bring it to Room 308?

C: Yes, of course. We provide very good room service.

G: Very good. When should we order our breakfast?

C: This is your doorknob menu. Just check the items for breakfast, mark down the time, and hang it outside your door before going to bed tonight.

G: Is there any other way of having room service?

C: Yes, sir. You may dial 1 to call the room service section directly to order your meal.

G: By the way, what should we do with the dishes when finishing eating?

C: Please leave them outside your room.

G: Thanks.

Dialogue 2   Order Breakfast

Scene: A guest (G) is calling the room service for the reservation of his breakfast. A clerk (C) answers the phone.

G: Hello, Room Service? This is Room 228. We'd like to order breakfast for tomorrow.

C: Yes, sir. What would you like?

G: We'd like to start with fruit juice. Fresh juice, please. Not canned or frozen.

C: All right, sir.

G: Good. And then eggs, tomatoes, toast and butter. Do you have different marmalades?

C: Yes, sir. We'll put a selection of preserves on your tray. And would you like tea or coffee?

G: Tea, please. With lemon, not milk.

C: Very good. And when is it?

G: Oh, about 7:30 would be fine.

C: Fine, and could you give me your name, sir?

G: It's John. Room 228.

C: Thank you, sir. Goodbye.

Dialogue 3   Offer Room Service in a Guest Room

Scene: A clerk (C) is serving the breakfast for a guest (G), and the guest wants to know how to deal with the tray when he's finished.

G: Please come in. Can you put it on the table over there? Thanks.

C: Shall I serve the soup, sir?

G: Er, yes, please.

C: Here you are, sir.

G: Thank you. That looks great.

C: Would you like to sign the bill, please, sir?

G: OK. Do you have a pen handy?

C: Here you are, sir.

G: Thanks…And where should I put the tray when I'm finished?

C: Oh, just call room service when you have finished; they'll come and collect the tray.
　　And you can also leave it outside the room, sir.

G: Thank you, I'll do that.

C: You're welcome. Goodbye, sir. Enjoy your meal.

G: Thank you. Goodbye.

Part Ⅲ   Useful Expressions

1. How to get room service.

　　We provide very good room service. Just dial 8 and order what you want.

　　Is there any other way of having room service?

　　What would you like?

　　Would you like anything else?

　　This is your doorknob menu. Just check the items for your breakfast. And then hang it outside your door.

2. Offer room service in the guest room.

　　Room service. May I come in?

　　May I serve soup now?

　　Would you like to sign the bill now?

　　You can leave the tray outside your room.

　　Please enjoy your meal.

Part IV Activities

1. Fill in the blanks with proper sentences.

A：Hello. Is this Room Service?

B：Yes，sir. May I help you?

A：Can I get something to eat at this time of night?

B：Yes，sir. _____1_____（你想要什么?）

A：I'll have a sandwich and milk.

B：_____2_____（您要哪种三明治?）

A：I'll take the steak，please.

B：White bread or rye?

A：White，please.

B：_____3_____（要烘烤吗?）

A：Toasted，please. _____4_____（要多久?）

B：It should be ready in five minutes.

A：Thank you.

B：Room Service.

A：_____5_____（请进）.

B：Shall I put it here?

A：Yes. On the table is fine.

B：Could you sign here，please?

A：Sure.

B：Good night.

2. Vocabulary：Get the correct meanings and learn them by heart.

Words and Expressions	Meanings	Words and Expressions	Meanings
doorknob		juice	
menu		marmalade	
section		preserve	
sign		tray	
lemon		soup	

3. Role-play.

Situation 1：Miss Bell orders some food and drinks for room service on the phone. Then a hotel staff member comes to the guest room with what the guest wants.

Situation 2：Mr. White wants to order room service for breakfast. He prefers English breakfast. Please help him.

4. Read and learn.

Full English Breakfast

Throughout Britain and Ireland，the full breakfast is well known. It is not usually eaten every day but saved for weekends and holidays. The term "full" comes from the fact the breakfast is，well，full of different foods. Full breakfast is served，as you would expect at breakfast time but is also popular throughout the day，often replacing lunch. It is particularly popular in bed and breakfasts，where no stay would be complete without one.

Breakfast may begin with orange juice，cereals，and stewed or fresh fruits(图 13-1). The heart of the full breakfast is bacon，eggs，and sausages (also called bangers in the U. K.). The dish is usually accompanied by grilled tomato，mushrooms，fried onions，toast，and marmalade. A cup of tea is a popular and traditional drink with breakfast，as is coffee. This breakfast is also called a fry-up. Since nearly all ingredients are prepared by frying. Other names it can go by include "a full Monty," supposedly named for British Army general Bernard Montgomery (nicknamed Monty)，who was said to have started every day with a full English breakfast during the campaign in North Africa during World War II. In Ireland，a full breakfast is sometimes referred to as a chub.

The origins of the breakfast are unclear and believed to have originated in rural England as a sustaining meal to carry workers through a long morning.

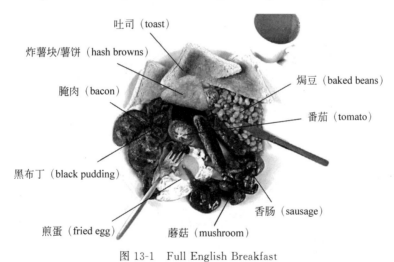

吐司（toast）
炸薯块/薯饼（hash browns）
腌肉（bacon）
焗豆（baked beans）
番茄（tomato）
黑布丁（black pudding）
香肠（sausage）
煎蛋（fried egg）
蘑菇（mushroom）

图 13-1　Full English Breakfast

Part V　Further Reading

Impressive Themed Hotel Rooms That You Can't Resist Booking(5)
Poseidon Undersea Resort｜Fiji

Poseidon Undersea Resort was supposed to open in 2008. But the project still hasn't started. Inspired by Poseidon and 20000 Leagues under the sea，the resort had an incredible vision. It was to feature a restaurant，bar，library，conference room，wedding chapel，spa，and luxury suite and guest rooms— all under the sea.

Can't wait for it to open? Take a look at a real underwater room(图 13-2)，the Muraka Suite at the Conrad. The Maldives' underwater suite will cost you ＄200000，but there are many perks，like falling asleep while fish-gazing.

图 13-2　A Underwater Room

Chapter 3　Food and Beverage Department

Restaurant of Crowne Plaza, Wuxi

Food and beverage department is the main service department to meet the needs of guests. Among the basic needs of tourists (hotel guests), food occupies the first place, and food is the first need for human life. Good catering and service is not only a hotel product, but also a tourism product. It is a resource that can attract tourists and establish a brand.

Hotel catering revenue is the main source of hotel operating revenue. The service place of the hotel food and beverage department is an ideal place for social gatherings. It has frequent contact with in-house guests and out-of-store guests day and night. Many guests often look at each other from a point of view and regard the impression of restaurants and bars as the impression of the whole hotel. The operation and management of the catering department and the quality of service are often related to the reputation and image of the hotel, and then affect the source of customers.

Unit 14
Table Reservations

Objectives

- Remember the specialized terms and expressions for table reservations.
- Understand working procedures for table reservations.
- Make table reservations for guests with different needs.

Lead-in

1. Discussion.

Why do we go to a restaurant for dinner? For food? For celebrations? For fun?...Share your own experiences with your classmates.

2. What can you see in the following four pictures?

(1) _____

(2) _____

(3) _____

(4) _____

Part I Background Knowledge

Brief Introduction to F & B

The food and beverage business has become one of the main businesses in a modern hotel. The restaurant of the modern hotel is not only the place for supplying food, but the place for leisure, banquet and communication. The products provided by food and beverage department are composed of tangible products with material forms and services with intangible forms. The tangible part of the catering products consist of the beverage, the appearance of the restaurant and the restaurant facilities, etc.; intangible product is the satisfaction of the guests, such as the reputation, the character, the atmosphere, the position, and the rank of the restaurant, etc. The tangible part and the intangible part of the catering products have different functions which cannot be replaced by each other and form the integral catering products.

Part II Situational Dialogues

Dialogue 1 Book a Table for Dinner

Scene: The reservationist (R) is booking a table for Mr. Smith (G).

R: Good evening. Rose Restaurant. Can I help you?

G: Hello. I'd like to make a reservation for a table in your restaurant.

R: For when, sir?

G: Thursday evening, say, around 7:30.

R: How many guests are there in your party?

G: There'll be six of us.

R: Smoking or non-smoking?

G: Oh, I didn't think about that. Non-smoking, I guess.

R: May I have your name, please?

G: It's Smith. Tom Smith.

R: OK, Mr. Smith. That's a party of six for Thursday evening at 7:30. Is that correct?

G: That's right. Thank you. Goodbye.

R: We are looking forward to seeing you on Thursday. Goodbye.

Dialogue 2 Fully Booked for a Table by the Window

Scene: Mr. Davis (G) would like to book a table by the window for tonight. But there is not any table available by the window for today. The reservationist (R) offers help for him.

R: Good morning. Rose Restaurant. May I help you?

G: Yes, I'd like to reserve a table for dinner.

R: What time would you like your table, sir?

G: I'm not sure, perhaps around 7 p.m. this evening.

R: Fine. How many people are there in your party?

G: Two.

R: Well, I'll reserve a table for two at 7 p.m., sir. May I have your name please?

G: Yes, Davis.

R: Thank you, Mr. Davis.

G: Oh, any chance of a table by the window? My friend loves the bird's eye view.

R: I see. But I am afraid there are no tables by the window available tonight, Mr. Davis. We have already received many bookings and I hope you'll understand.

G: I do, but we really enjoy having dinner by the window. What a pity!

R: I'm sorry about that. Well, Mr. Davis, if you don't mind, you can book a table for tomorrow night. I see there is a table by the window available for tomorrow.

G: Great. Then I will have a reservation for dinner tomorrow night at 7 p.m. Thank you so much.

R: You are welcome. See you tomorrow, Mr. Davis.

Dialogue 3   Book a Private Room for Dinner

Scene: Mr. Matthews (G) is calling the reservations to reserve a private room for dinner. The reservationist (R) receives his request.

R: Good morning. Rose Restaurant. Advance Reservation. Can I help you?

G: Yes, I'd like to reserve a table for this evening, please.

R: For how many persons, please?

G: A party of eight.

R: At what time can we expect you?

G: Oh, at 6:00 tonight.

R: Would you like a table in the main restaurant or in a private room, sir?

G: A private room will be better.

R: May I have your name and telephone number, please?

G: Sure. It's Matthews and my number is 13561877699.

R: So, it's Mr. Matthews, a private room for 6:00 this evening.

G: That's right.

R: Thank you for calling. We're looking forward to seeing you. Goodbye.

G: Goodbye.

Dialogue 4   A Face-to-face Reservation for a Banquet

Scene: A guest (G) is booking a banquet for a birthday party. The reservationist (R) is communicating with him.

G: Excuse me; I want to order a banquet. Who is in charge of it?

R：It's me，sir. What can I do for you?

G：I want to hold a birthday party in your restaurant next Sunday evening，about 6：00 p.m. Will that be OK with you?

R：Yes，sir. It's our pleasure. How many tables do you want to order? And may I know your name and telephone number?

G：Tim Wang. About 5 tables. And my telephone number is 13812812009.

R：How much would you like to pay for each table?

G：I'll pay up to 2000 yuan for each table.

R：Yes，Mr. Wang. We have three kinds of menus for this price. You can choose one of them and also you can decide the menu by yourself.

G：OK. Let me see.

R：We offer dishes with Huaiyang，Sichuan and Cantonese flavors. Here are the menus.

G：OK，I'll choose Huaiyang cuisine.

R：Ok，Mr. Wang. Will you please pay the deposit?

G：How much should I pay now?

R：One thousand yuan，please.

G：Here is 1000 yuan.

R：Thanks. Here's the receipt. Do you have any other requirements for the birthday party?

G：Please prepare happy songs as the background music，but don't make it too noisy.

R：No problem，Mr. Wang. Bye-bye.

Part Ⅲ   Useful Expressions

1. Ask about table reservation details.

May I help you?

When would you like your table，please?

May I have your name，sir?

How do you spell it，please?

What time would that be?

How many people are there in your party?

I'd like to confirm your reservation.

2. Tell the reservationist about the details.

I'd like to reserve a table for four.

I'd like to book a private room for ten，please.

At seven o'clock tomorrow evening.

We would like a table in the corner.

We prefer a tale by the window.

Do you have a dress code?

Part Ⅳ　Activities

1. Translate the following sentences into Chinese.

（1）I'd like to reserve a table for two at seven tonight.

_____

（2）When would you like your table?

_____

（3）How many persons are there in your party?

_____

（4）We'd like a table with a view of the garden.

_____

（5）Do you have a dress code?

_____

2. Vocabulary: Get the correct meanings and learn them by heart.

Words and Expressions	Meanings	Words and Expressions	Meanings
reserve		dress code	
banquet		in charge of	
private room		flavor	
anniversary		Cantonese	
non-smoking		receipt	
invoice		discount	

3. Role-play.

　　Situation 1: Mr. Smith is calling to book a table by the window at the non-smoking section. And he would celebrate their 15th anniversary of wedding with his wife.

　　Situation 2: Ms. Ma wants to book a private room for a dinner party. She and her colleagues will welcome some newcomers in her team.

4. Read and learn.

Table Reservation Procedure for Restaurants

A. Answering the telephone.

　　Good (morning/afternoon/evening). Roof Top Restaurant, Albert speaking. How may I help you?

B. Acknowledging a reservation request.

　　Certainly, Mr. David Smith. (use name if known)

Yes, of course, sir/madam. (use name if known)

C. Taking the table reservation details.

May I have your name, please?

When would you like to book your table?

A table for how many guests?

Where would you like to sit?

D. When you check the reservations book.

Please excuse me, (name), while I check the reservations.

Please allow me to put your call on hold, while I check the availability.

Just one moment, please (name), while I see what we have available.

E. Returning to the caller.

I'm sorry to keep you waiting, (name).

Sorry to keep you on hold, (guest Name).

May I have your mobile number, please?

F. Confirming the details.

May I repeat the table reservation details? A table for (2) (this afternoon/on Sunday, 31 October) at (6.00 p.m.) in the name of (Mr. Davis). And your (telephone number) is (13851516666). Is that correct?

G. Saying goodbye.

Thank you very much for calling, Mr. Davis. We look forward to seeing you then. Have a great day.

H. When a table is not available.

I'm afraid we don't have a table at that time. Would (7:30) be suitable?

I'm afraid we don't have a table available at that time. But there is a table available (say where) then. Would that be suitable?

I. Offering an alternative.

May I help you to reserve a table at another of our restaurants instead?

Perhaps you'd like to have (lunch) in the (Wok Restaurant), where there will be a buffet this afternoon.

J. Reconfirming a restaurant table reservation request.

I would like to reconfirm your reservation for a table for two this afternoon at 6:00 p.m.

Thank you very much for making the reservation and we look forward to being of service to you.

A birthday cake with the words "Happy Birthday to Betty" has been arranged for tonight.

Part V　Further Reading

Beijing Roast Duck

Beijing Roast Duck is a world-famous dish. It originated in the Southern and Northern Dynasties in China. It was a palace food at that time. Beijing duck is made of high-quality ducks, roasted by charcoal fire of fruit wood. The color is rosy, and the meat is fat but not greasy. It is crispy outside and tender inside. Beijing Roast is known as the "world delicious" with its red color, tender meat, mellow taste, fat but not greasy characteristics. It is very popular with foreigners.

Unit 15

Seating Guests

Objectives

- Master specialized terms and expressions for seating guests.
- Understand the working procedures for seating guests.
- Seat guests without reservations flexibly.

Lead-in

1. Think it over and share your ideas with your classmates.

What kind of welcome ceremony do you prefer? Describe an experience that you are warmly welcomed by someone or you welcome somebody warmly.

2. Match the pictures with the words given below.

A. fork   B. service plate   C. wine glass   D. soup spoon

(1) _____

(2) _____

(3) _____

(4) _____

Part I　Background Knowledge

Job Description of Restaurant Hostess

The restaurant hostess is the first employee to interact with arriving guests as they enter the restaurant. She should make it sure to provide proficient and professional food & beverage service to the guests by meeting and also exceeding their expectations.

The hostess is also responsible for welcoming the guests by greeting them as per the standards and responding to customer queries by resolving issues in a timely and efficient manner to ensure customer satisfaction.

Part II　Situational Dialogues

Dialogue 1　Seat Guests with a Reservation

Scene: A waitress (W) receives a guest (G) who has a table reservation.

W: Good evening, Ma'am. Good evening, Sir. Welcome to our restaurant.

G: Good evening. We would love a table for two.

W: Sure. Do you have a reservation with us?

G: Yes. My family name is Wang.

W: OK, Mr. Wang. Let me check. One moment please. Found it. A table for two at 6 p.m. This way, please. I will show you to your table.

G: Thank you.

W: My pleasure. Enjoy your dinner, please.

Dialogue 2　Welcome a Guest Who is Coming Alone

Scene: A host (H) receives a guest (G) who comes to the restaurant alone.

H: Good afternoon, ma'am. Welcome to Rose Restaurant.

G: Thanks.

H: May I ask if anyone is joining you?

G: No. I've come alone.

H: Where would you prefer to sit? What about a seat by the window?

G: I prefer to sit near the air-conditioner.

H: OK. This way, please.

G: Thanks.

Dialogue 3　Share a Table

Scene: A host (H) receives guests (G) who would not like to share a table with others.

H: Good evening, sir.

G：Good evening. Could you find us a table for two, please?

H：I'm afraid all our tables are taken, sir. Could you wait in line until a table is free, please?

G：Well, how long will it take?

H：About fifteen minutes, sir.

G：That's a bit too long.

H：Would you mind sharing a table, then?

G：Well, we'd rather wait.

H：All right. Could you take a seat over there? I'll inform you when a table is free.

G：That's fine.

(*fifteen minutes later when a table is free*)

H：Excuse me. We have a table for you now, sir. This way, please.

G：OK.

Dialogue 4　Seat Guests without a Reservation

Scene：Helen（H）is the reservation clerk for Minor Shanghai Restaurant. She is receiving a guest（G）without a reservation.

H：Good evening. Do you have a reservation, sir?

G：No, I'm afraid I don't.

H：How many people are there in your party, sir?

G：Four.

H：I'm sorry, but you will have to wait for about 45 minutes before a table is free. May I have your name, please, sir?

G：Yes, Henry Smith.

H：Mr. Smith, would you like to have a drink in the lounge in the meantime?

G：That's a good idea. Thank you.

(*almost 40 minutes later, the waiter comes from the restaurant*)

H：We can seat your party now, Mr. Smith.

G：Good!

H：Please step this way. Will this table be all right, Mr. Smith?

G：Yes, thank you.

H：Here is the menu, sir. I'll return in a few minutes to take your order.

G：Please be quick as soon as possible. We're terribly hungry.

H：OK.

Part III　Useful Expressions

1. Welcome guests.

Good evening, sir/madam.

How many guests are there in your party?

Where would you like to sit?

This way, please.

A waiter or waitress will come soon to take your water.

2. Seat a guest who has a reservation.

Do you have a reservation?

May I have your name, please?

I'm afraid the tables you reserved are not ready yet.

I will show you to your table.

3. Seat a guest who hasn't made a reservation.

Would you mind sharing a table?

I will inform you when a table is free.

Would you like to have a drink while waiting for a while?

I am very sorry to have kept you waiting.

Is this table fine?

How about this table?

Will this table be all right?

What about tables near the stage?

I'm sorry, sir. The window tables have all been taken.

Here is the menu. Take your time, please.

Part IV   Activities

1. Vocabulary: Get the correct meanings and learn them by heart.

Words and Expressions	Meanings
by the window	
host	
waiter	
reservation	
hostess	
lounge	
waitress	

2. Role-play.

Situation 1: John Brown comes to your restaurant with his two friends without a reservation. Please welcome them and seat them.

Situation 2: John Brown comes to the Rose Restaurant with his family for dinner. He made a reservation for a table by the window. Please welcome them and seat them.

3. Read and learn.

Basic Menu Knowledge for F&B Service Staff

All the F&B service staff shall be thoroughly familiar with all beverage items listed on the menu, their origins and how they are prepared and served. Although some items may not be listed on the menu, all staff shall have a basic but correct knowledge of most popular beverage items which exist but are not necessarily served in the outlet.

Additionally, every staff member shall have a basic knowledge of wines regarding the most common origins and appellations as trained by the Food & Beverage Management Team and according to the Hotel's sales mix. Below are some of the basic knowledge and skills which the hotel F&B service staff should possess.

The food and beverage service staff should be able to describe the dishes on the menu to the guest in a simple and clear way.

Should be able to pronounce all food items in the menu accurately.

Should know the ingredients and cooking methods of all items on the menu.

Should know the preparation time of each dish.

Should know what condiments and/or sauce to serve with the dish.

Should know how the dish should be served.

Should know which section of the kitchen produces the dish.

Should know what are the daily specials and seasonal ingredients.

Should know what item is out of stock.

Should know which are the signature dishes of the restaurant.

Should know what else can be proposed to guest in terms of cooking method besides the one listed and make appropriate recommendations.

Should know the selling price of the dish.

Should know the portion size of each dish and give appropriate suggestions to the guest especially those served in pieces.

Should know the history and the place of origin of the ingredients or dishes.

Part V   Further Reading

How to Be a Great Host or Hostess in a Restaurnt

As a host or hostess, you are the first and last person guests see at a restaurant. Because of this, you must always be alert, attentive and efficient. Keeping the restaurant orderly, making sure guests are happy, and keeping track of what's going on at each table are just some of the ways you can keep your guests happy.

Staying Organized

(1) Make sure you have all of the supplies you need before your shift starts.

（2）Keep track of each section.

（3）Communicate with your servers.

（4）Walk the floor to keep track of the tables.

（5）Help to clear and set tables when necessary.

Greeting Guests

（1）Greet guests with a smile and welcome them to the restaurant.

（2）Ask how many people are in the party.

（3）Ask customers if they have a seating preference.

（4）Answer the phone promptly.

（5）Maintain your composure even if the restaurant gets hectic.

（6）Show your guests to their table.

（7）Make sure your guests are seated comfortably.

Unit 16

Taking Orders

Objectives

- Remember the specialized terms and expressions for taking orders.
- Recommend dishes for guests according to their requirements.
- Deal with situations when taking an order in a professional way.

Lead-in

1. Think it over and share your ideas with your classmates.

What kind of food would you like to eat? Western food or Chinese food? Why? Can you cook some dishes by yourself?

2. Match the words with the pictures.

    A. milk shake   B. hamburger   C. cheesecake

    D. ice cream   E. salad   F. steak

(1) _____

(2) _____

(3) _____

(4) _____

(5) _____

(6) _____

Part I　Background Knowledge

Job Description for Restaurant Captain

A restaurant captain is responsible for promoting and ensuring guest satisfaction, maintaining a safe and sanitary work environment and ensuring only the highest quality products are being served.

A restaurant captain should also build guest loyalty and gather constructive feedback to ensure satisfaction of every guest. Handling daily team member relations, and encouraging problem-solving by team members through proper training and empowerment are also restaurant captain's responsibilities.

Part II　Situational Dialogues

Dialogue 1　Today's Special

Scene: A waitress/waiter (W) is taking an order for a guest (G) in a western restaurant.

W: May I take your order, sir?

G: Yes. What do you have for today's special?

W: We have filet steak and lamb chop.

G: Oh, I'll take filet steak.

W: How would you like your steak done? Rare, medium or well-done?

G: Medium, please.

W: Would you like your steak with baked potatoes or French fries?

G: Baked potatoes, please.

W: Would you care for a salad, sir?

G: Yes. What kinds of salads do you have?

W: We have mixed salad and tomato salad.

G: A mixed salad is fine.

W: And what would you like to drink with your meal?

G: I'd like to order wine.

W: The wine list is on the last page of the menu, sir.

G: Ah, here we are.

W: Take your time.

G: A Marseilles, please.

W: Let me repeat your order, sir. You would like to have filet steak, baked potatoes, a mixed salad, and a Marseilles. Is it correct?

G: Exactly.

W: OK. Enjoy your meal, sir.

Dialogue 2　Order Chinese Food

Scene: A waitress/waiter (W) is taking an order for a guest (G) in a Chinese restaurant.

W: Are you ready to order now, sir?

G: No, I'm still reading the menu. You see, this is my first trip to China. I don't know much about Chinese food.

W: Chinese food is divided into eight big cuisines, such as Cantonese cuisine, Sichuan cuisine, Shandong cuisine, Huaiyang cuisine, etc. Our restaurant is famous for Sichuan cuisine.

G: I have heard Sichuan food is spicy and hot.

W: Yes.

G: But I really like spicy food. Could you recommend something?

W: What about the boiled fish with pickled cabbage and chili sauce, and the spicy Sichuan bean curd? They are our specialties.

G: OK. I'll have them.

W: OK, sir. Would you like some vegetables for your lunch?

G: Oh, yes. Could you make a suggestion for us?

W: Yes. How about spicy cabbage of Sichuan style? It's our chef's recommendation.

G: That's fine. I'll have a try.

W: Sir, your dishes will take 15 minutes to prepare. While waiting, would you like anything to drink?

G: Two glasses of white wine, please.

W: Yes, sir. The boiled fish with pickled cabbage and chili sauce, spicy Sichuan bean curd, spicy cabbage of Sichuan style and two glasses of white wine.

G: That's right.

W: Just a moment, please.

Dialogue 3　Recommend Dishes

Scene: The waiter (W) recommends dishes for the guests (G).

W: Good evening, sir. Here is the dinner menu.

G: Thank you.

W: Please take your time.

(*after a while*)

W: May I take your order now?

G: Yes, we would like to have the Great Fun for two, please.

W: I'm afraid this is for four or five persons.

G: Well, can't you make it for two only?

W: I'm afraid not, sir. The Great Fun is for a minimum of four to five persons, so I think it will be too much for you.

G：I see. What do you recommend then?

W：I would recommend the Friendship，which is for two persons.

G：It contains fried chicken，doesn't it? How many pieces are there per serving?

W：Four pieces，sir.

G：OK. We'll take the Friendship.

Dialogue 4　Recommend Chinese Dishes

Scene：A waitress（W）is recommending dishes for her foreign guests（G）.

W：Good evening. Are you ready to order?

G：I think so，but could you tell me about this dish?

W：Certainly. This is called "shui zhu yu"（水煮鱼）. It is fish slices in spicy soup.

G：That sounds very nice. What would you recommend to go with it?

W：Stir-fried green beans are called "si ji dou"（四季豆）. That dish is very popular.

G：We don't eat much Chinese food so we will take your advice.

W：I can also recommend a home-style fried tofu dish called "jia chang dou fu"（家常豆腐）.
　　It's a home-style bean curd with some vegetables.

G：That sounds good too.

W：And would you like noodles or rice to go with that?

G：Let's have rice.

W：What would you like to drink with your meal?

G：Some water would be great.

W：Mineral water，purified water，or carbonated water，like Evian?

G：Mineral water，please.

W：Certainly. Is there anything else I can get you?

G：Yes，could you get some green tea for us?

W：Sure. Your food will be here soon. Can you use chopsticks?

G：Yes，not very well，but we can. Thank you.

W：If you need a fork and knife，let me know. Enjoy your meal.

Part Ⅲ　Useful Expressions

1. Ask guests to order.

　　May I take your order now?

　　Are you ready to order now，sir?

　　Please have a look at the menu first.

　　What would you like to have today?

2. Ordering food.

　　What is the specialty of the restaurant?

What is today's special?

Can I have the same dish as that?

I have to avoid food containing fat (salt/sugar).

Do you have vegetarian dishes?

How do you like your steak?

Well-done (Medium/Rare), please.

I'm afraid that this vegetable is not in season. Would you like to try something else?

Would you like some dessert?

What would you recommend? I prefer something light.

3. Ordering drinks for the meal.

Would you like something to drink before dinner?

What kind of drinks do you have for an aperitif?

May I see the wine list?

I'd like to have some local wine.

Part Ⅳ　Activities

1. Share your idea with your friends.

Do you like the following food? Why? And what is your favorite food?

steak

toast

dumplings

hot dog

pizza

porridge

2. Vocabulary: Get the correct meanings and learn them by heart.

Words and Expressions	Meanings	Words and Expressions	Meanings
Today's special		baked potato	
filet		salad	

Continued

Words and Expressions	Meanings	Words and Expressions	Meanings
lamb		aperitif	
chop		wine	
rare		menu	
medium		Marseilles	
well-done		cuisine	
spicy		recommend	
pickled cabbage		chili sauce	
chef's recommendation		bean curd	
fried chicken		slice	
mineral water		purified water	
carbonated water		chopsticks	

3. Role-play.

Situation 1: John Brown and his family want to try some Chinese dishes. He asks the waitress for advice.

Situation 2: John Brown and his wife want to have some western food. Please help them to order some food and drinks.

4. Read and learn.

Key terms or Jargon used in Food and Beverage Service

A la carte: A menu that offers prices of each food and beverage item on an individual basis.

Room Service Menu: Menu fixed for room service or in-room-dining department.

Fixed Menu: A menu that doesn't change every day.

Cyclical Menu: Menu that changes daily for a certain number of days e. g. from Monday to Friday, and then repeats again.

Table d'hote (Buffet Menu): A Menu that offers several courses at one fixed price, generally known as buffet menu.

Baked: Cooked by dry heat in an oven.

Boiled: Cooked by boiling.

Braised: Browned in a small amount of fat.

Broiled: Cooked by direct heat from above and below.

Grilled: Cooked on a grid over direct heat.

Mise-en-place: Mise-en-place means "putting in place" and the term denotes the preparation of a work place for ultimate smooth service. e.g. The waiter makes sure that this station has been efficiently prepared for service.

Chafing dish: It is a hollow ware used to keep the food warm usually in buffet service.

Cover: Cover is the space on the table allotted for table-wares to the guest to consume his/her meal. The standard size of the cover is $24'' \times 18''$.

Poached: Cooked in enough simmering liquid to cover the food.

Roasted: Cooked uncovered without water added in an oven using dry heat.

Sauteed: Browned in a small amount of oil or fat.

Steamed: Cooked in steam.

Stewed: Simmered slowly in enough liquid to cover the food.

Part V Further Reading

Man-han Banquet

Man-han Banquet(图 16-1) is one of the grandest meals ever documented in Chinese cuisine (see the picture below). It consists of at least 108 unique dishes from the Manchu and Han Chinese culture during the Qing Dynasty, and it was only reserved and intended for the emperors. The meal was held for three whole days, across six banquets.

图 16-1 Man-han Banquet

Unit 17

Serving Dishes

- Be able to use specialized terms and expressions for serving dishes.
- Understand the working procedures of serving dishes.
- Deal with problems when serving dishes flexibly.

Lead-in

1. Think it over and share your ideas with your classmates. Which is your favorite dish?

A. steamed fish

B. braised fish

C. stewed fish

D. boiled fish slices with
pickled cabbage and chili

2. Match the words with the pictures.

A. Dumplings　　B. Zongzi　　C. Tangyuan

D. Stuffed bun　　E. Deep-fried dough strips　　F. Sweet and sour pork ribs

(1) _____　　　　(2) _____　　　　(3) _____

(4) _____　　　　(5) _____　　　　(6) _____

Part I　Background Knowledge

Job Description for Restaurant Waitress/Waiter

A restaurant waitress/waiter should ensure that all guests are served to the hotel standards in the restaurant/bar/lounge areas. He/She should also display highest standards of hospitality at all times within all food and beverage areas.

He/She is also responsible for taking orders for, serving food and beverages to guests in a friendly, timely and efficient manner.

Part II　Situational Dialogues

Dialogue 1　Take Your Plate

Scene: A waiter (W) is serving a guest (G) his/her meal.

W: Your steak, salad and red wine, sir. Please enjoy your meal.

G: Thank you.

W: Excuse me. May I take your plate, sir?

G: Sure. Go ahead, please.

W: May I show you the dessert menu?

G: OK.

W: Here you are.

G: Let me see. I'd like to have a chocolate pudding, please.

(*after 3 minutes*)

W: Your chocolate pudding, sir. Shall I bring your coffee now, or later?

G: Later. Thank you.

Dialogue 2　Chinese Dinner Custom

Scene: A guest (G) is wondering about Chinese dinner custom. A waiter (W) is explaining to her.

W: Here are your cold dishes, ma'am.

G: Thank you. I wonder why a Chinese dinner always starts with cold dishes instead of hot courses. Could you explain that to me?

W: Of course, ma'am. It's a custom in our country to serve cold dishes first as they have been prepared beforehand, but hot courses usually won't be prepared until the dinner starts.

G: Oh, I see. The chef in your country is in the habit of preparing cold dishes first.

W: I'm afraid that's not exactly right. We Chinese people usually regard the dinner party as an occasion for a friendly chat.

G: Yes, I quite agree. But what's that to do with cold dishes first?

W: Well, people usually talk more and eat less at the beginning of the dinner. So if hot courses are served beforehand, they will get cold soon and much of their flavor will lose then. For this reason, cold dishes are usually served first.

G: Oh, I see. Thank you.

W: You are welcome. Have a good time!

Dialogue 3　Wrong Dish

Scene: A guest (G) was given a wrong dish. A waiter (W) is checking the serving procedure and communicating subsequent compensation matters with the guest.

G: Excuse me, sir. I ordered the hairy crab but you gave me the green crab.

W: I'm sorry, sir. I'll get to check with our chef and the headwaiter.

(after 3 minutes, the waiter comes back)

W: I'm awfully sorry. There must have been some mistakes. I do apologize for giving you the wrong dish. I'll change it immediately for you. The crab will take 15 minutes to prepare. Would you take some complimentary drink while waiting?

G: I'm afraid I don't have enough time to wait for the next dish. I have an appointment at 7:30 in my room. Now it's 7:15.

W: Oh, you are staying at our hotel. Mr. ...

G: Bell, Henry Bell in Room 608.

W: Oh, Mr. Bell. I shall ask the Room Service to serve you a snack at 9:00 tonight and you'll have your favorite hairy crab. It's all on the house. And now try the green crab if you don't mind. We'll cross the green crab off the bill.

G: That's fine. Thanks.

W: Thank you for telling us, Mr. Bell. I assure you it won't happen again. Please take your time and enjoy yourself. And I hope you will have a good time in our hotel.

Part Ⅲ Useful Expressions

1. Serving dishes.

Here is your food.

Here is the fried beef with green pepper and onion.

May I serve it to you now?

Please take your time and enjoy yourself.

Your meal will be ready soon.

Shall I serve it now, or after your dinner?

This food is best eaten while hot.

2. Ask guests about their feelings about the meals.

Are you enjoying your meal?

Is everything to your satisfaction?

How is your meal?

How is everything?

I'm afraid there is a mistake.

I'll get you the headwaiter.

3. When mistakes occur during the meal.

I'll change it immediately for you.

I'm awfully sorry. There must/might have been some mistakes.

I'm afraid I don't have enough time to wait for the next dish.

It's complimentary.

That would be on the house.

It's free of charge.

Part Ⅳ   Activities

1. Vocabulary: Get the correct meanings and learn them by heart.

Words and Expressions	Meanings	Words and Expressions	Meanings
soft boiled egg		table d'hote (buffet menu)	
hard boiled egg		chop	
scrambled egg		buffet service	
omelettes		chili	
a la carte		cold dishes	
stew		rib	
grill		crab	
steam		on the house	
braise		complimentary	

2. Role-play.

Situation 1: Mr. Smith, a diner at Rose Restaurant, is asking the waiter how to eat Beijing Roast Duck.

Situation 2: A guest is having her last dish, but she finds it is different from what she has ordered. The waiter apologizes for the error and offers to replace it. The guest says she has no time to wait for the ordered dish, for she has an important appointment. The waiter says the guest can try this dish if she doesn't mind, and he will cross the dish off the bill.

3. Translation practice.

(1) 我们有蛋炒饭。您想要些吗?

_____

(2) 北京烤鸭配有蔬菜.

_____

(3) 饺子是我们的传统食物.

_____

(4) 酸辣汤值得尝一尝,是中国的特色汤。(hot and sour soup)

_____

(5) 这是本餐厅的特色菜,请您慢慢品尝。

_____

4. Read and learn.

F&B Service Techniques for waitress and waiters

A. How to handle trays.

All trays must be clean and stain-free.

Never overload or stack up too high.

Small service tray should be carried with one hand.

Big tray must be always carried with two hands.

Place the left hand under the center of the tray with fingers spreading out comfortably.

Heavy, high and hot items must be close to your body.

Don't walk too fast and always use tray mat or liner for balance.

B. How to serve snacks.

Snacks are served for every guest who is seated for a drink.

All bar snacks are free of charge and refillable. (Depending upon your hotel policy.)

Serve the bar snacks right away when guest is seated.

Quantity of bar snacks differ on the number of guests.

Always make sure there are enough paper tissues while serving snacks.

Part V Further Reading

Serving Dishes

Serving dishes refers to the service of delivering the food and beverage to table, and serving the guest during the meal. Influenced by the western food service, Chinese food service gradually adopts the buffet meal or the divided meals. Good service requires the staff to combine the standard operation skills and courteous service etiquette to maximize customer satisfaction. In this service period, safety and hygienic problem of the food and beverage service should be paid much more attention; if meeting the special circumstance, the staff also should have the strong adaptability.

Unit 18

Drinks

Objectives

- Remember the specialized terms and expressions of drinks.
- Help guests to order drinks according to their requirements.
- Deal with various situations of ordering drinks.

Lead-in

1. Think it over and share your ideas with your classmates.

What is your favorite drink? Why do you like it?

2. Discuss with your classmates.

In the food and beverage service, the profit of the beverage service is quite high. Especially, the hotel bar is the business site for providing alcoholic and non-alcoholic beverages for customers.

Q1: What drinks do restaurants and hotels often provide to their guests?

Q2: What do people usually drink during Chinese banquets?

Q3: What do people usually drink when they are eating western food?

3. Match the names with the drinks on the pictures.

　A. beer　　B. mineral water　　C. wine　　D. milk　　E. orange juice

　F. coffee　　G. Chinese Baijiu　　H. cocktail　　I. whisky　　J. champagne

　　　　(1) _____　　　　　　(2) _____　　　　　　(3) _____

(4) _____   (5) _____   (6) _____

(7) _____   (8) _____   (9) _____   (10) _____

Part I   Background Knowledge

Job Description of Barman/Bartender

A bartender is responsible for preparing and serving drinks to customers. He/She also should be able to mix and match ingredients in order to create classic and innovative drinks in accordance with customers' needs and expectations. The purpose of this position is to interact with the hotel guests and ensure they have a great experience at the bar or lounge.

A bartender should maintain positive guest interactions while accurately mixing and serving beverages to guests in a friendly and efficient manner.

Part II   Situational Dialogues

Dialogue 1   Order Something to Drink

Scene: Two guests are in the bar. They want to check the drink list and have something to drink.
W: waitress/waiter; G1: Guest A; G2: Guest B

W: Good evening. Would you like something to drink?

G1: Yes, but give us a couple of minutes to look through the drink list first.

W: Sure, sir. Please take your time.

G1: Let's see. Champagne, beer, whisky, cocktail ... I'd like some iced beer. What about you, Ann?

G2: I don't drink at all. Do you serve soft drinks?

W: Certainly, ma'am. We have a variety of soda water and fruit juice.

G2: What kind of fruit juice do you have?

W: Plum juice, orange juice, carrot juice, pineapple juice, lime juice and tomato juice.

G2: I'll have lime juice.

W: Any special brand of the beer, sir?

G1: Budweiser. One will do.

W: Good. A can of Budweiser and a glass of lime juice. Just a moment, please.

Dialogue 2   Try Something Typically Chinese

Scene: William (W) is the bartender of Wuxi Intercontinental Hotel. She is receiving reservation request from a guest named Gerry (G).

G: Is this the bar?

W: Yes, come in, please.

G: What kind of wine do you offer?

W: Here is the wine list.

G: Thank you.

W: What would you like?

G: I'd like to try something typically Chinese today.

W: Would you like something like Wuliangye?

G: Is there anything else beside Wuliangye?

W: Yes, we have eight famous liqueurs. I suggest you try a cup of Fen Wine from Shanxi.

G: Fen Wine from Shanxi?

W: Right. It's a mixture of real Chinese ingredients.

G: Let me try it.

W: Here it is, sir.

G: Oh, it's excellent.

Dialogue 3   Take Orders and Serve Beers

Scene: A guest (G) wants to try something new for his night drink. A clerk (C) is giving him some advice.

C: Good evening, sir. What would you like to drink?

G: I'd like to have a change tonight. What's your suggestion?

C: Why not try something typically Chinese?

G: Good. I'll have a try of the local beer.

C: Tsingtao beer is very popular here.

G: I'll have Tsingtao beer, please.

C: OK. One Tsingtao beer.

G: Right.

C: I'll be right back.

Dialogue 4　Recommend Tea

Scene: A guest (G) wants to have tea. A clerk (C) is introducing different kinds of tea to her.

C: Good evening, Ma'am. Welcome to our teahouse.

G: Good evening. I'd like some tea, please.

C: What tea do you prefer?

G: Green tea, please.

C: We have Dragon Well Tea from Hangzhou and Biluochun Tea from Jiangsu. Do you want to have a try?

G: I've heard a lot about Dragon Well Tea. So, Dragon Well tea, please. By the way, is there any black tea in China?

C: Yes. The most famous black tea is Oolong. But green tea is the wisest choice especially in summer.

G: Oh, what's jasmine tea?

C: It's a kind of green tea with the smell of jasmine. Beijingers like it very much.

G: I see. I will try Dragon Well Tea and Jasmine Tea.

C: Would you like your tea now?

G: Yes, please.

Part Ⅲ　Useful Expressions

1. Taking orders for drinks.

What would you like for a drink?

With or without ice, sir?

An aperitif or some white wine?

Its alcohol content is very low. It's a fancy aperitif.

We serve cucumber juice, orange juice, carrot juice and tomato juice. All of them are spot-squashed.

2. Beer.

It's our self-brewed draught beer.

Do you prefer bottled or canned?

Make me a cold beer.

Make sure it is well chilled.

I stick to my usual, one pint of Carlsberg.

132

3. Some other drinks.

We don't need soda in our red wine. However, please do add some Sprite and ice for the ladies.

I'll have a Brandy, please.

We'd like to have a change, but we don't quite know what to drink today.

Part IV   Activities

1. Vocabulary: Get the correct meanings and learn them by heart.

Words and Expressions	Meanings	Words and Expressions	Meanings
beverage		Chinese Baijiu	
brandy		cocktail	
alcoholic		whisky	
non-alcoholic		champagne	
Chinese banquet		soda water	
mineral water		pineapple juice	
lime juice		ingredients	
brand		Tsingtao beer	
Biluochun Tea		Dragon Well Tea	
jasmine tea		aperitif	
spot-squashed		red wine	

2. Role-play.

Situation 1: You are a waitress in a hotel. Mr. Bellow, a diner at Jasmine Restaurant, is ordering some drinks of foreign brands.

Situation 2: You are a waiter in a hotel. Mr. Green has a whole-day sightseeing in Guangzhou in May, and he returns to the hotel. Feeling rather exhausted, he enters the bar to relax and asks you for some suggestions.

3. Translation practice.

(1) How would you like it, straight up or on the rock?

(2) Would you like to try some Chinese alcohol?

(3) "Mao Tai" is one of the most well-known Chinese spirit.

(4) It's rather strong, but never goes to the head.

(5) If we add ice, the taste will be spoiled.

---

4. Read and learn.

What are Alcoholic Beverages?

Alcoholic Beverages are portable liquid which contain 1% to 75% ABV of liquor. They are produced by the introduction of yeast for fermentation.

Yeast is added into substance such as grapes, grains, barley, fruits, sugarcane and rice and then distilled. The alcohol content is measure as "Alcohol by Volume" which is abbreviated as "ABV".

Fermented Beverages (9%-16% ABV)

Fermented beverages, as its name suggests are those types of alcohol which are prepared with a fermentation process. During this process the sugar is converted to ethanol and carbon dioxide with the help of yeasts. Some examples of fermented beverages are beer, champagne, and wine etc.

Distilled Beverages (17%-75% ABV)

Distilled beverages are also called as spirits. These types of alcohol are produced by the distillation process where juice or other liquids already fermented are evaporated by boiling and then collected via process called condensation. There is a large variety of liquors produced with this process like Whiskey, Brandy, Gin, Vodka, Tequila, Rum etc.

Fortified Drinks (up to 20% ABV)

Fortified drinks are those who have been fermented, distilled and then finally be "fortified" to increase its alcohol content by adding additional alcohol. This is done to achieve a balance in flavor and liquor content. Some examples of fortified drinks are port wine, Madeira, chamomile etc.

Liqueurs or Creams (15%-30% ABV)

These are alcoholic beverages which are made from distilled spirits, which is then flavored with cream, spices, nuts, herbs, coffee, chocolate etc. Some examples are Sheridan's Coffee Liqueur, Baileys Irish Cream Liqueur, Amarula Fruit Cream Liqueur etc.

Types of Alcoholic Beverages

Type	Made from
wine/champagne	grapes
beer	grain
whiskey	grain, barley, corn
brandy	grain
Aperitif/digestif	grapes

Continued

Type	Made from
liqueur	grain, grapes, fruits, sugarcane
spirits	grain, grapes, fruits, sugarcane
sake	rice

Part V   Further Reading

Cocktail

Cocktail is a mixed drink originating in the United States and served as an appetizer(图 18-1). It generally has a basis of gin, whisky, rum, or brandy combined with vermouth or fruit juices and often flavored with bitters or grenadine. It is blended by stirring or shaking in a vessel containing cracked ice. The term is also applied to nonalcoholic beverages served as appetizers, e. g., tomato juice cocktail, and also to mixed, cut-up fruits and to shellfish and oysters served with a sharp sauce.

图 18-1   An example of a cocktail

Unit 19

Dealing with Complaints in the Restaurant

Objectives

- Be able to use the specialized expressions for dealing with complaints.
- Understand the working procedures in settling complaints.
- Deal with guests' complaints professionally.

Lead-in

Compare the formal and informal expressions for gratitude and apology，and then practice using them in your conversations with your partners.

gratitude 致谢	expressions	answers
formal expressions	Thank you so much.	It is my pleasure.
	I really appreciate it.	You are most welcome.
	Thank you for all you have done.	My pleasure.
informal expressions	Thanks a lot.	You are welcome.
	Thanks.	Any time.
	I own you one.	No problem.

apology 致歉	expressions	answers
formal expressions	My sincere apologies.	Think nothing of it.
	Please forgive me.	Don't give it another thought.
	I apologize for the inconvenience.	These things happen.
	We are terribly sorry.	Thank you.
informal expressions	Sorry.	It is okay.
	I am so sorry.	No worries.
	Oh，wow. Sorry，man!	That's cool.

Part I　Background Knowledge

Job Description for Silver Service Waiter

A silver Service Waiter/Waitress is generally a more experienced waiter that specializes in serving food, using a fork and spoon, from platters directly to the guests' plates at the table.

He or she is responsible for providing food and beverage service to guests according to established standards, policies and procedures. Also, he or she should provide a courteous and professional service at all times. He/She bears the responsibility for all duties prior to and after service, in order to ensure maximum guest satisfaction at all times.

Part II　Situational Dialogues

Dialogue 1　Bring the Guest with Wrong Order

Scene: A waiter (W) serves the wrong dish to a guest (G).

W: Excuse me, ma'am. Here is your steak.

G: Wait a minute. This is not what I ordered. I ordered salmon.

W: I am sorry. I apologize for bringing you the wrong order. We will prepare your salmon right away.

G: Oh, well, thanks.

W: Is there anything else I can assist you with?

G: No, thank you.

W: Your salmon will arrive shortly. Once again, I apologize for bringing you the wrong order.

Dialogue 2　The Fish is not Fresh

Scene: A guest (G) found the fish in his dish is not fresh. He is complaining to a waiter (W) and the waiter is trying to comfort him.

G: Excuse me.

W: Yes, sir?

G: The fish is not fresh.

W: Oh, I am sorry that your fish is not fresh. Please accept our apologies. We will cook another one for you right now. And you will not be charged for it.

G: Good.

W: Is there anything else I can get for you?

G: No, thanks.

W: Once again, please accept our apologies. I will get that order for you right away.

Dialogue 3   I Have been Waiting for My Food for So Long!

Scene： Two guests are complaining about the long time they have been waiting for their food. A waiter is communicating with them to make some compensation for their wasted time.

W：waiter；G1：Guest A；G2：Guest B.

G1：I am hungry. Where is my food?

G2：Excuse me.

W：Yes，sir?

G2：My food still has not arrived. I have been waiting for almost half an hour.

W：I am so sorry your food hasn't arrived yet，sir. Please accept our apologies. I was just in the kitchen and saw your pasta being cooked. It is going to be ready in five minutes. Will you accept a complimentary hot beverage as our way of apologizing? Here is our beverage menu.

G2：We appreciate that. We will have two cappuccinos.

W：All right. Is there anything else I can assist you with?

G1：No，thank you.

W：Your drinks will arrive shortly. Once again，I apologize for your food being late. Thank you for your patience. I will return with your pasta shortly.

Part III   Useful Expressions

1. accepting a complaint.

　　I'm terribly sorry.

　　I can't tell you how sorry I am.

　　Oh，dear. I'm really so sorry.

　　I'm so sorry，sir.

　　I'm very sorry to hear that，ma'am.

2. responding to complaints.

　　I'll see to resolving the problem right away，ma'am.

　　I'll take care of that right away，ma'am.

　　I'll see to it immediately.

　　I'll check about it and get back to you.

　　I sincerely apologize for the oversight，sir. I'll have a complimentary bottle/entrée delivered immediately. Please accept it with our compliments.

Part IV   Activities

1. Vocabulary：Get the correct meanings and learn them by heart.

Words and Expressions	Meanings	Words and Expressions	Meanings
salmon		resolving the problem	

Continued

Words and Expressions	Meanings	Words and Expressions	Meanings
assist		fresh	
complimentary		deliver	
hot beverage		apologize	
cappuccino		breakage	
pasta		complaint	

2. Role-play.

Situation 1: A guest ordered a tofu dish. But it smells terrible. Then he complains about this dish. You, as a waitress/waiter, deal with this complaint politely.

Situation 2: The guest complains about the wrong number on the bill. Please deal with it carefully.

3. Read and learn.

Handling Guest Complaints and Problems
in a Restaurant/Coffee Shop

A. Approach the guest and ask politely if there is a problem.

Excuse me, may I help you, Mr. Samuel? (Listen with concern and empathy).

Stay calm. And never argue with the guest.

Be aware of the guest's self-esteem. Show a personal interest in the problem. Try to use the guest name frequently.

Tell the guest what can be done. Offer choices. Don't promise the impossible, and don't exceed your authority.

Set an approximate time for completion of corrective actions. Be specific, but do not underestimate the amount of time it will take to resolve the problem.

Monitor the progress of the corrective action done to resolve the guest complaint.

Follow up. Even if the complaint was resolved by someone else, contact the guest to ensure that the problem was resolved satisfactorily.

Restaurant staff should take corrective actions without any hesitation.

B. Apologizing and taking action as per issue.

I'm so sorry (about this), Mr. Samuel.

I'm terribly sorry (about this).

Please accept (our/my) sincere apologies, Mr. Dull.

C. For complaints about the food.

Shall I bring you another juice?

I'll bring you another one right away.

I'll change it right away.

I'll speak to the chef, and see what we can do.

Would you like your steak cooked a little more?

Would you like to order something else instead?

I'll have the kitchen prepare another one. Would you like some wine while you are waiting?

D. About the service.

I'll look into the matter at once.

I'll see about your order right away.

Excuse me, Mr. Bernard. It will be about another 15 minutes for your chicken soup to get ready.

Your food will be ready in about 15 minutes. (Apologize if there has been a delay.) Thank you for your patience.

E. About the table.

I'm afraid all the tables (near the pool/lake view area) are already taken. I'll let you know as soon as when one is free.

I'm sorry, but the restaurant is very full at the moment. This is the only table I can offer you.

F. Spillages.

Let me help you, Mr. Wilson. /Allow me, Mr. David.

I'll fetch you a towel/some water.

I do apologize for the accident, Mr. Langer. May I have it dry-cleaned for you?

Part V Further Reading

北京奥运主题歌"You and Me"

you and me, from one world

heart to heart

we are one family

you and me

from one world

heart to heart

we are one family

for dreams we travel

thousands of miles

we meet in Beijing

come together

the joy we share

you and me

from one world

forever we are one family

Unit 20

Paying the Bill

Objectives

- Use the specialized terms for settling the bill properly.
- Understand the working procedures of cashier service.
- Settle bills in different ways for guests.

Lead-in

1. Translate the following paragraph and share your understanding with your classmates.

After finishing the dinner, the guests can pay at the Cashier Desk of the restaurant. If the guest stays at the hotel, he/she can sign the bill, and make payment at one time until checking out. The food and beverage department of the restaurant often accept payment in cash, by credit card or by traveler's check. The waiter should settle the bill accurately, promptly and politely.

2. What can you see in the following pictures? Do you usually use them for payment?

Part I Background Knowledge

Job Description for Food and Beverage Director

The Director of Food and Beverage is responsible for coordinating all phases of group meeting/banquet functions held in the hotel, coordinating these activities on a daily basis and assisting clients in program planning and menu selection.

He/She also bears the responsibility of soliciting local group food and beverage business, maintaining the services and reputation of the hotel and acting as a management representative to group clients.

Part II Situational Dialogues

Dialogue 1 Pay the Bill in Cash

Scene: A guest (G) has finished his meal and is calling the waiter (W) for bill.

G: Waiter, please!

W: Yes, sir. Can I help you?

G: Can I have the check?

W: Yes, sir. Here it is.

G: Would you please explain this entry to me?

W: That's your soup.

G: Oh, I see. And what about the service? Is it included?

W: Yes. Here it is. Five percent for service charge.

G: So it totals $ 52.8. Here is the money. Keep the change. Thank you for your nice service.

W: Thank you, sir. Goodbye.

Dialogue 2 Sign the Bill

Scene: A guest (G) has finished his meal and wish to sign the bill. A waiter (W) is checking his room card and number.

G: Please bring the bill, waiter!

W: Yes, one moment, please.

(*The waiter brings the bill.*)

W: Here you are, sir.

G: How much do I have to pay?

W: It totals 280 yuan. And how would you like to make your payment, sir?

G: I'd like to sign the bill.

W: Yes, sir. May I look at your room card and passport?

G: Certainly. Here you are.

W: Please write down your room number here, too.

(*The waiter checks the name, room number and signature carefully, and does not find anything wrong.*)

W: Thank you. I hope you've enjoyed your meal.

G: The meal was delicious.

W: Thank you for your appreciation.

Dialogue 3　Pay the Bill by Credit Card

Scene: A waiter (W) is helping a guest (G) to pay his bill by credit card.

W: Here is the bill, sir.

G: I'd like to pay with a credit card. Do you accept credit cards?

W: Yes, we accept American Express, Visa and Master card.

G: That's fine. I will pay my bill with Master Card.

W: May I have a imprint of your card, sir?

G: Yes, of course. Here you are.

W: Thank you. I'll be right back.

(The waiter comes back with the card.)

W: Sorry, sir. The card is expired. Do you have another card?

G: Yes, you may try this Visa Card.

W: (The waiter comes back with the receipt.) It's OK. Could you please sign your name here?

G: Yes.

W: Thank you. Here is the bill and receipt. Have a nice day!

Dialogue 4　Use the Discount Card and Voucher

Scene: A guest (G) wants to use discount card and voucher when paying the bill. A waiter (W) is explaining the related regulations to him.

G: Please bring me the bill, waiter!

W: Yes. How would you like to pay for it, sir?

G: I'd like to pay by cash, but I've got discount card and voucher.

W: I'm sorry. Discount card and voucher can not be used together.

G: Well, use the vouchers first. Do you have more vouchers?

W: Sorry. If you use discount card next time, we'll send you more vouchers.

G: All right.

Part Ⅲ　Useful Expressions

1. When a guest wants to pay the bill.

　　Waiter! The bill/check, please.

　　Bring me the bill, please.

May/Can I have the bill/check, please?

Would you please bring us the bill, please?

You may pay at your table, sir.

Would you care to have one bill or separate bill?

It's my treat. One bill, please.

I'd like to settle my bill, please. How much is it?

2. Tell guests the amount.

Your bill comes to $ 65.

There is an extra 10% service charge.

The meal totals $ 58.

Here is your change of $ 15.

Keep the change, please.

3. After paying the bill.

I hope you enjoyed your meal.

I don't think the bill is right. Can you check it again?

May I have the receipt/invoice, please?

It's ripping off.

Can I have any coupons for the next time?

Part Ⅳ   Activities

1. Vocabulary: Get the correct meanings and learn them by heart.

Words and Expressions	Meanings	Words and Expressions	Meanings
cash		voucher	
credit card		treat	
sign the bill		go dutch	
American Express		separate bill	
Visa		rip off	
Master card		coupon	
receipt		Ali pay	
discount card		WeChat	

2. Role-play.

Situation 1: Mr. Green, one diner at Miracle Restaurant, would like to pay his bill in cash.

Situation 2: Mr. White, one guest at California Restaurant, would like to pay his bill by credit card.

3. Read and learn.

Different Types of Food and Beverage Services in Hotels ｜ Restaurants
French Service

French Service is a very detailed and highly skilled type of service. It is a very elaborate and expensive type of service.

The chefs demonstrate culinary skill, by preparing meals in front of the guests.

Normally all fine dining restaurants follow this type of service.

VIPs and VVIPs are also given this kind of service style.

Plated entrees are served from the right, all other courses from the left. Beverages are served from the right. French Service style is very expensive because it involves professional waiters to serve properly and slowly. The ambience and decor of the restaurant are always in high luxury.

4. Translation practice.

(1) I'm afraid we cannot accept foreign currency as payment here.

_____

(2) Could you pay at the Cashier Desk at the entrance, please?

_____

(3) Excuse me, but I think you've overcharged me.

_____

(4) I'm sorry for the mistake. Here is the right change.

_____

(5) Could you sign the bill here, please?

_____

Part Ⅴ ｜ Further Reading

Going Dutch

Going dutch is a slang term indicating that each person participating in a shared activity pays for himself or herself, rather than one person pays for the others. There is a delicate etiquette surrounding going Dutch. It is widely accepted in some situations, such as between non-intimate friends or less affluent people, but can be considered stingy in other circumstances, such as on a romantic date or at a business lunch.

Chapter 4　Convention and Recreation Center

A Meeting Room of Wuxi Hubin Hotel

The conference service represents the image of the whole hotel. When organizing meetings, it should be strict and orderly.

A Swimming Pool of a Marriot Hotel

Recreation is an activity of leisure. The "need to do something for recreation" is an essential element of human biology and psychology. Recreational activities are often done for enjoyment, amusement, or pleasure and are considered to be "fun".

Unit 21

Convention Service

- Book conference rooms for guests.
- Offer services before the meeting.
- Offer services during the meeting.

Lead-in

Match the names with proper pictures.

A. white board
B. television
C. conference room
D. PA system (public-address system)
E. laptop computer
F. multimedia projector

(1) _____

(2) _____

(3) _____

(4) _____

(5) _____

(6) _____

Part I Background Knowledge

The setup of a meeting room can make a difference between a productive meeting and a non-productive one. The setup you choose depends on how many people will attend and the purpose of the meeting.

There are many basic seating arrangements. Whichever you choose, it should promote open discussion among attendees as well as with the discussion leader. Bearing these points in mind, the four most common setups include:

A. Theater.

Chairs in rows, facing front, no tables. It is the arrangement of choice if the meeting features a number of speakers, a performance, or audiovisuals, and if you want to maximize the space in a room(图 21-1).

B. Classroom.

Attendees are seated in rows of tables placed facing the front. This is an excellent setup if there will be a number of speakers or extensive note-taking(图 21-2).

图 21-1 Theater

图 21-2 Classroom

C. Conference Style.

Participants sit on three sides of a rectangular table and focus on a power figure at the head. This arrangement makes it easy for participants to see one another and also provides a writing surface. Conference style(图 21-3) is best for under 30 people.

D. U-shape.

It is one of the most popular seating arrangements for groups of less than 30 participants (图 21-4). This seating style, optimal for training sessions and speaker presentations, positions the leader either in the middle of the connecting end of the U or in the middle of the U. The openness of this setup gives attendees a sense of freedom that encourages wider participation.

图 21-3 Conference Style

图 21-4 U-shape

Part Ⅱ　Situational Dialogues

Dialogue 1　Book a Conference Room

Scene: A staff (S) receives a guest (G) who wants to book a conference room.

S: Good morning, Ms. Lee, how can I help you?

G: Well, would you please find a room for our business meeting?

S: Certainly. How many people will attend the meeting?

G: About six.

S: OK, I see. We have a conference room on the executive floor, which can hold 8 people. Would you like to have a look?

G: Yes, please.

S: This room can seat up to 8 people and we will offer tea free of charge for your meeting. Since you are on the executive floor, you can use the meeting room two hours for free per day.

G: That's great.

S: When will you use it, Ms. Lee?

G: Um, we'll start the meeting at 9 o'clock tomorrow morning.

S: May I know how long you will use the meeting room?

G: About 3 hours, and how much does it cost for the extra hours?

S: The charge for the extra 1 hour is RMB 200 yuan, Ms. Lee.

G: That's fine.

S: And do you need anything else for the meeting, like projector or white board?

G: No, thanks.

S: Ms. Lee, we'll arrange the meeting room for you. The meeting time is from 9:00 to 12:00 tomorrow morning. We'll offer complimentary tea for your meeting, and the meeting room rent is RMB 200 after discount.

G: That's right. Thank you.

S: You are welcome.

G: Goodbye.

S: Goodbye and have a nice day.

Dialogue 2　Book an Auditorium and Some Facilities for the Conference

Scene: A staff (S) receives a guest (G) who wants to book an auditorium and some facilities.

G: We're going to hold a conference next Saturday. I'd like to book some facilities and personnel for it.

S: No problem, sir. Here is the rate list.

G: Thank you.

S：You are welcome，sir. Next Saturday ... that's May 6th，isn't it?

G：Yes. We need an auditorium for 60 people，a projector and a video camera.

S：60 people ... I think a small auditorium will be enough.

G：Good idea. I also need two messengers.

S：I see. Could you please sign here? And also，your telephone number，please.

G：OK.

S：Thank you，sir. Everything will be ready by Friday afternoon. Could you come and check it then?

G：Sure. Thanks.

S：You're welcome，sir. We're looking forward to serving you.

Dialogue 3　Service for Refreshments of Tea Break

Scene：When the break starts，attendees go for refreshment.

W：Waiter；G：Guest

W：Ladies and Gentlemen，we're providing you with dessert and beverages here. Hope you enjoy them.

G：What kind of dessert do you provide?

W：A wide variety，such as pumpkin pie，apple tart with whipped cream，and so on.

G：All right，I'd like this one. It looks good.

W：Here is the tray. Help yourself，please.

G：Is this green tea?

W：Yes. It is Longjing Tea. Have a try，please.

G：Thanks.

Part Ⅲ　Useful Expressions

1. Book/reserve a conference room.

  A：Jennifer，could you book us a conference room?

  B：What time?

  A：1：00 to 3：00 tomorrow afternoon.

  B：All settled.

2. Call for meeting.

  A：Have you received the call for meeting?

  B：Not yet. I thought there would be no meeting today.

3. Calendar event.

  A：The best way to notify a meeting is to set it up as a calendar event.

  B：I know. But people are used to the phone notification or email.

4. Miss the meeting.

  A：Once people get used to the calendar，they will see how convenient it is. They will never miss another meeting.

B: You're right.

5. Meeting agenda.

A: Kate, has the meeting agenda been printed?

B: Not yet, because I found a problem in it.

6. Revise the agenda.

A: Yesterday we have talked about the attendance record, but it wasn't mentioned.

B: Oh yes, we are supposed to discuss that today. We should put it in. I will revise the agenda.

7. No mobile phones.

A: Elsie, remind me to announce a new rule before the meeting.

B: Okay, but what is it?

A: No mobile phones. I'm really fed up with people receiving calls.

8. Put off/postpone the meeting.

A: Martin, I think the group meeting today has to be put off.

B: What's the matter?

A: I heard Tina and Kate went to the headquarter for a meeting.

B: Really? I'm in complete agreement to put off the meeting.

Part Ⅳ　Activities

1. Vocabulary: Get the correct meanings and learn them by heart.

Words and Expressions	Meanings	Words and Expressions	Meanings
attendee		video camera	
theater		auditorium	
participant		dessert and beverages	
U-shape		pumpkin pie	
white board		conference room	
training session		executive floor	
presentation		charge	
complimentary		rent	
projector		apple tart with whipped cream	

2. Role-play.

Situation 1: Mr. Green is calling to reserve a meeting room for his company next Friday morning. There will be 30 people attending the meeting. And he needs some facilities for the meeting. He also wants the hotel to prepare a tea break for the conference.

Situation 2：Ms. Taylor and the hotel clerk are talking about the arrangements. With a banquet，the conference will be held next Saturday afternoon. There will be 11 people. Please help Ms. Taylor to make some choices for the conference and the banquet.

3. Translation practice.

（1）我们下周六要开一个为期一天的会议，需要一间能容纳 50 人的礼堂。

_____

（2）我们要为会议预定一些设施和人员。

_____

（3）我们需要一个投影仪和笔记本电脑，另外周一需要一名同声传译。

_____

（4）您准备如何支付，用支付宝、微信还是信用卡？

_____

（5）Please wait a moment，sir. I have to check the computer records.

_____

Part V   Further Reading

Gross Things in Your Hotel Room You Should Avoid（1）

—By Jake Schroeder

Many of us see vacation as a time to kick back，unwind and maybe enjoy some of the perks of a hotel stay. For those of us who worry about cleanliness，however，a hotel might not be the most relaxing place to sleep. With so many people passing through a room，some things are bound to get dirty — but you'd at least hope they change the pillowcases，right? Prepare to discover the most germ-laden items in the average hotel room.

A. Carpeting.

When staying at a hotel，not many people think about what they're walking on. That's why the carpet is the dark horse of the dirty objects in your hotel room—but when you think about it，it's not hard to see why(图 21-5).

图 21-5   A Small Piece of Carpet in a Hotel

How many people have traipsed through in their shoes? Or walked around in their bare feet? Sure, housekeeping service people vacuum after every visit, but rarely if ever does a hotel carpet get a deep clean between guests. If you're concerned about other people's germs, you might want to keep your socks on.

B. Pillowcases.

This dirty hotel item is one of the most shocking—and might make you want to swear off of hotels forever. That's right; according to a study, many cleaners don't change pillowcases when re-making beds. Instead, they toss the pillows aside while changing sheets and then put the pillows right back where they were(图 21-6).

图 21-6　Pillows in a Hotel

Unit 22

Recreation and Fitness Service

Lead-in

1. Match the pictures with the words given below.

A. swimming pool	B. fitness center
C. table tennis room	D. bowling
E. yoga	F. billiard room
G. tennis	H. playing golf
I. barber's	J. spa

(1) _____

(2) _____

(3) _____

(4) _____

(5) _____

(6) _____

　(7) _____　　　(8) _____　　　(9) _____　　　(10) _____

2. Discussion.

　　Q1：Name as many sports as you can.

　　Q2：What is your favorite sport? Why do you like it?

Part Ⅰ　Background Knowledge

Here are some terms related to recreation center. Try to remember the following terms.

beauty salon	美容中心
swimming pool	游泳池
sauna	桑拿
clinic	医务室
multifunction hall	多功能厅
chatting bar	聊天吧
reflexology service center	足浴中心
table tennis room	乒乓球室
billiards room	桌球室
fitness center	健身中心
tennis court	网球场
chess and cards room	棋牌室

Part Ⅱ　Situational Dialogues

Dialogue 1　At the Recreation Center

Scene：A receptionist（R）receives a guest（G）who wants to take some exercise and show him some detailed information about the facilities.

R：Good afternoon. Can I help you?

G：I'd like to take some exercises. Could you tell me what facilities you have here?

R：Certainly, sir. We have a well-equipped gym with all the latest recreational sports, apparatus, such as exercise bicycles, weights, swimming pools, tennis courts and so on. You may find more details in this map.

G：That sounds terrific!

R：Then we have an excellent sauna, with a free supply of towels and soap.

G：Great! I'd like to go swimming. By the way, do you sell swimming trunks here? I've left mine at home.

R：Yes, you can find them at the shop nearby.

G：Thank you very much.

Dialogue 2　Serve Guests with Kids for Swimming

Scene：A recreation clerk（RC）receives a guest（G）with kids for swimming.

G：Hello. Could I get some towels for the kids?

RC：Of course. Could I see your room card?

G：Sure!

RC：Thank you and here are your towels.

G：Can we swim in the pool now?

RC：Of course. Please give me your key and I will fetch your items. I have already prepared a few bottles of water and some fruit by that table over there.

G：Thank you very much.

（after the guests finish swimming）

RC：Here are your items. Would you mind filling out this feedback form? I would be really appreciative.

G：Of course. I would be happy to fill it out.

RC：Thank you. Please enjoy your stay in our hotel.

Dialogue 3　Bowling

Scene：A recreation clerk（RC）receives a guest（G）who wants to play bowling.

RC：Good evening, sir. May I help you?

G：What time will you close?

RC：We are open till 12：00 p.m.. But the service hours of bowling are from 9：00 a.m. to 8：00 p.m.

G：How much do you charge for an hour?

RC：Thirty yuan an hour. Would you like to have a try?

G：Sure.

RC：Thank you, sir. How would you like to pay, in cash or signing the bill?

G：Sign the bill, please. Here is my room key.

RC：Thank you. We will keep your room key here. You can get it back after playing. Special bowling shoes are available here. Would you please tell me your size?

G：Oh, size 41.

RC：Here are the shoes. Lane 6, please.

Dialogue 4　At the Beauty Saloon

Scene：A guest（G）wants her hair shampooed，head and face massaged. The Hairdresser（H）serves the guest.

H：Good evening, madam. Would you like your hair done?

G：Yes. I'd like my hair shampooed.

H：Take the seat, please.

G：Well, I'd like my head and face massaged, too.

H：All right, madam. Please have a look. Is this the style you want?

G：Yes, it looks great. Thank you.

Part Ⅲ　Useful Expressions

1. Introduce facilities.

> Our gym has all the latest exercise equipment, including exercise bikes.
>
> There are personal trainers and coaches standing by to show you what to do.
>
> We offer yoga, pilates, martial arts, and Tai chi classes.
>
> How about bowling?

2. Offer suggestions for sports.

> You'd better do some stretches before you work out.
>
> You'd better warm up first.
>
> Can you show me how to use this machine?
>
> Sit here and pull this bar down to your shoulders.
>
> Please wipe off the machine after use.
>
> Do you need some help using that machine?
>
> This exercise is good for your back.
>
> This exercise will help build your shoulders.
>
> I would suggest a yoga/an aerobics class.

Part Ⅳ　Activities

1. Vocabulary：Get the correct meanings and learn them by heart.

Words and Expressions	Meanings	Words and Expressions	Meanings
gym		golf course	
apparatus		basketball court	
sauna		supervision	
massage		refreshment	
bowling		snack	

Continued

Words and Expressions	Meanings	Words and Expressions	Meanings
Jungle gym		feedback	
locker		appreciative	
squash court		beauty salon	

2. Role-play.

Situation：A guest with a ten-year-old girl wants to swim in the swimming pool. Please tell them the instructions that the parents should take care of their own children in the swimming pool. Then help the guests to do the preparations for swimming.

3. Translation practice.

（1）你们酒店附近有高尔夫球场吗？

_____

（2）健身房的服务要额外收费吗？

_____

（3）请您将自己的东西放在储物柜。

_____

（4）It sounds that playing table tennis is good for our health.

_____

（5）I'm afraid you cannot wear your own slippers in the gym.

_____

Part Ⅴ Further Reading

Gross Things in Your Hotel Room You Should Avoid（2）

—By Jake Schroeder

A. Light Switches.

It might not surprise you that light switches tend to be hotspots for bacteria accumulation. After all，everyone needs to turn the lights on，and not everyone washes their hands on a regular basis. In a hotel room，you'll want to be especially wary of the light switches on your bedside lamp(图 22-1).

图 22-1 A Lamp in a Hotel

The good news is that dirty switches are an easy fix; all you need are some alcohol wipes. Stick these in your luggage and wipe the switches when you first arrive. You're in the clear!

B. Welcome Cards.

Most hotels provide welcome cards(图 22-2) or booklets inside their rooms. These can be quite useful, giving you information on everything from the Wi-Fi password to the best pizza place in town. Before you peruse the pamphlet, however, consider cleaning it first.

图 22-2   A Welcome Card in a Hotel

参 考 文 献

[1] 旅游饭店职业英语编委会. 旅游饭店职业英语(中级)[M]. 3 版. 北京：旅游教育出版社,2010.

[2] 上海旅游行业饭店职业能力认证系列教材编委会. 旅游饭店实用英语[M]. 北京：旅游教育出版社,2011.

[3] 高文知. 酒店情景英语[M]. 2 版. 北京：北京大学出版社,2017.

[4] 张丽君. 酒店英语[M]. 2 版. 北京：清华大学出版社,2018.

[5] 李光宇,瞿立新. 酒店前厅与客房部运行与管理[M]. 北京：高等教育出版社,2015。

[6] 3A 系列教材编写组. 酒店英语与国际服务文化(上册)[M]. 北京：机械工业出版社,2021.

[7] 云丽虹. 实用酒店英语[M]. 上海：上海交通大学出版社,2015.

[8] 欧阳莉,范洪军等. 酒店英语实训教程[M]. 长沙：湖南大学出版社,2018.

[9] 韩雪. 酒店英语听说强化教程[M]. 4 版. 北京：旅游教育出版社,2021.

[10] 王青,沈建龙. 酒店英语实训教程[M]. 北京：中国人民大学出版社,2016.

[11] 金利. 终极酒店英语话题王：最新实用场景＋必知必会词句[M]. 上海：华东理工大学出版社,2018.

[12] 肖璇,郭一新,王大维. 现代酒店英语实务教程[M]. 北京：世界图书出版公司,2021.

[13] 朱华. 酒店英语(视听版)[M]. 2 版. 北京：北京大学出版社,2021.

[14] 雷乾乾,华国梅,夏季. 酒店英语实训活页教程[M]. 北京：旅游教育出版社,2020.

[15] 魏凯,草常玲,宿翠萍. 旅游职业道德[M]. 3 版. 北京：中国旅游出版社,2021.